JOY for LIFE

Connie Cross

CONNIE CROSS

Joy for Life

Unless otherwise indicated, all Scripture quotations are taken from the Holy Bible, New Living Translation, copyright © 1996, 2004, 2007 by Tyndale House Foundation. Used by permission of Tyndale House Publishers, Inc., Carol Stream, Illinois 60188. All rights reserved.

Scripture quotations marked NIV from the THE HOLY BIBLE, NEW INTERNATIONAL VERSION®, NIV® Copyright © 1973, 1978, 1984, 2011 by Biblica, Inc.® Used by permission. All rights reserved worldwide.

Scripture quotations marked KJV taken from the Holy Bible, King James Version. (Public Domain)

Scripture quotations taken from the Amplified® Bible, Copyright © 2015 by The Lockman Foundation Used by permission." (www.Lockman.org)

All rights reserved. No portion of this book may be reproduced, stored in a retrieval system, or transmitted in any form or by any means-electronic, mechanical, photocopy, recording, or any other- except for brief quotations in printed reviews, without the prior permission of the publisher.

ISBN: 978-1-940682-4-57
Copyright © 2016 by
International Women's Discipleship.
All Rights Reserved
Printed in the United States of America

Table of Contents

Introduction 7

WEEK ONE: A Taste for Sweets 9

WEEK TWO: Anticipation 13

WEEK THREE: Autumn 17

WEEK FOUR: Bluebonnets 21

WEEK FIVE: Change of Plans 25

WEEK SIX: Changes 29

WEEK SEVEN: Crayons 33

WEEK EIGHT: Dancin' Shoes 37

WEEK NINE: Determination 39

WEEK TEN: Do You See the Reflection 43

WEEK ELEVEN: Doing Music 47

WEEK TWELVE: Don't Miss the Flight 51

WEEK THIRTEEN: Facing Mountains 55

WEEK FOURTEEN: Fishing 59

WEEK FIFTEEN: Have a Blessed Day 61

WEEK SIXTEEN: He Knows My Name 65

WEEK SEVENTEEN: Here Comes the Judge 69

WEEK EIGHTEEN: Home 73

WEEK NINETEEN: Hot Air Balloon Ride 77

WEEK TWENTY: Hungry and Thirsty 81

WEEK TWENTY-ONE: Hunting 85

WEEK TWENTY-TWO: Hurricanes 87

WEEK TWENTY-THREE: I Gained an Hour 89

WEEK TWENTY-FOUR: I Hear Christmas Music 93

WEEK TWENTY-FIVE: I Remember a Stormy Night....97

WEEK TWENTY-SIX: Inspired 101

WEEK TWENTY-SEVEN: It Was a Crash 103

WEEK TWENTY-EIGHT: Make Up Your Mind 107

WEEK TWENTY-NINE: My Broken Arm 111

Table of Contents

WEEK THIRTY: My Life is a Book 113

WEEK THIRTY-ONE: Never Alone 117

WEEK THIRTY-TWO: Noise 121

WEEK THIRTY-THREE: Perception 125

WEEK THIRTY-FOUR: Planting Seeds 129

WEEK THIRTY-FIVE: Procrastination 131

WEEK THIRTY-SIX: Rejoice 133

WEEK THIRTY-SEVEN:: Restored 137

WEEK THIRTY-EIGHT: Seeing 139

WEEK THIRTY-NINE: Starting and Finishing 143

WEEK FORTY: Stormy Days and My Nose 147

WEEK FORTY-ONE: Strong Bones 151

WEEK FORTY-TWO: Symphony 155

WEEK FORTY-THREE: Texting 159

WEEK FORTY-FOUR: The Abandoned Raft 161

WEEK FORTY-FIVE: The Broken Cup 165

WEEK FORTY-SIX: The Powerful Word of God 169

WEEK FORTY-SEVEN: The Statistics Tell Us 173

Joy for Life

WEEK FORTY-EIGHT: To Tell the Truth....................175

WEEK FORTY-NINE: Toastmasters............................179

WEEK FIFTY: Unexpected Surprise............................183

WEEK FIFTY-ONE: What A Difference a Day Makes 187

WEEK FIFTY-TWO: Words are Powerful....................191

About the Author...195

Introduction

It started out as weekly email devotions, initially to those in our own congregation who desired to receive it. Wanting to find a way, in our ever-so-busy lives, to inspire and encourage others regularly, I thought it would be fun to send a Scripture, along with a personal note or story, and a word of encouragement each week. The intent was to share a little *Joy for Life* each week for one year. As time went by, the readers began to invite friends and family to also receive the devotion. It has extended into China, Lebanon, and the Czech Republic. This book of 52 weekly entries has been published by requests from the readers of the emails. At the time of this printing, we are in our third year of writing weekly devotions.

My sincere prayer is that everyone who reads these simple thoughts will receive encouragement and inspiration, and experience a little more *Joy for Life*. If you have never experienced the joy that comes from having a dynamic and personal relationship with Jesus Christ, or if you have lost the joy you once experienced, I pray that the thoughts shared in this book will ignite a desire in your heart and

Joy for Life

mind that will not be satisfied until you've experienced a fresh and dynamic relationship with Him...the Giver of Joy!

Joyfully,

Connie Cross

A Taste For Sweets

I have a problem! I wish I could change, but I have a problem. I have a desire for too many desserts. It has been my weakness for as long as I can remember. I've always loved cookies and pie, cake and ice cream, cobbler, candies, and brownies. When I was a toddler, there were some people in our church that had a little gas station and store. They would give a little brown sack of candy to me and a little sack of candy to my big brother when we would go by their place. I would quickly eat all of my candy, and then beg my brother for some of his. I don't think I was really greedy, I just wanted a little more candy. After all, I was just a little kid! I'm all grown up now, but I still have this tendency. If there are M&M's, pecan pralines, Mounds, peanut brittle, or peanut patties, I cannot stay away. A few years ago, a co-worker, knowing my fondness for Snickers bars, came in to work and said "I brought you some Snickers bars—a large one, and a small one." A little later in the day she came by and wanted to know which one I had eaten that day. I told her, "Both!" Just a few weeks ago at Christmas, the women's board of our church

Joy for Life

presented me with a beautiful bouquet of Payday candy bars, knowing I love those. Yes, I enjoy having something sweet to eat. What about you?

When I think about my relationship with God, I think of it as being sweet. Having a candy bar is enjoyable, but having a taste of the presence of God in my life is incredible. Having a sweet relationship with the Almighty God and Creator is beyond description. Having a touch of His love in my hungry heart fills me with joy that cannot be measured. The Bible tells us in Psalm 119:103-105,

> How sweet your words taste to me; they are sweeter than honey. Your commandments give me understanding; no wonder I hate every false way of life. Your word is a lamp to guide my feet and a light for my path.

God's Word is full of sweet treasures for each one of us. His Word speaks to us of His great love. He speaks to us of His righteousness and holiness. He tells us about His justice. He tells us about His amazing mercy and grace. We read and learn about His provision, His miracles, and His desire to be the Lord of our life. We learn about His plan for us now, and what He desires for our future. We can enjoy so much sweet fellowship with God. Listen to what Jeremiah said in the scripture:

> When your words came, I ate them; they were my joy and my heart's delight, for I bear your name, O Lord God Almighty (Jeremiah 15:16 NIV).

Amazing, isn't it? Jeremiah learned to (spiritually) eat God's Word, and it became his joy and heart's delight. I have a longing to "eat the Word" and have God's Word so alive in my life that I am a walking, living testimony of His grace and goodness.

There are so many things I want to write about, but I bought some Girl Scout cookies at church last Sunday. I think I should check them out.

Joy for Life

Anticipation

What are you anticipating today? You may be reading this on Sunday morning, and you are anticipating a dynamic church service. You may be reading this on Monday or Tuesday, and you are anticipating a great day at work or school. You may be anticipating starting a new school year, or starting a new job. You may be anticipating getting a new piece of furniture or jewelry this week. For a mother-to-be, there is great anticipation, knowing that a little baby is on the way, soon to make a grand entrance. Maybe you're anticipating trying out a new recipe and can't wait to check it out. In hot, dry weather, when we hear a forecast of rain, we begin to anticipate the much needed moisture. In the fall, we anticipate the holidays. Thanksgiving is close, and then comes Christmas, and we all anticipate the wonder and beauty of the holiday season. Terry and I love to travel, and we love the anticipation of a trip. If it's a road trip or a fly-away trip, the anticipation of the journey is fun, even before we reach the destination. Anticipation…it's a great thing! Anticipation defined is, "the act of looking forward; especially pleasurable expectation." Anticipation is expectation, excitement. It's fun to be in a state of anticipation, when you know something good is going to happen.

A research study was done that involved a group of people who were awarded a meal at a fancy French restaurant. Those selected were given the opportunity to go for the dinner at different times, such as "now," "tonight," "tomorrow," or "next week." The meal was available any time, but most of the people wanted to wait and put it off a few days. It was determined that part of the joy of the fancy French restaurant experience was the anticipation of the event. These people were anticipating a great night, and realized that part of the joy before the actual event was the anticipation of what was ahead.

When we look around our world today, we hear so much negative news. Is it for real? Yes, we know it is real, and there are many adverse things happening around us. There are trials we face, and there are struggles we endure. There are crooked people in the world that have no values or morals. However, I'm determined to live in anticipation! I'm determined to look forward to what is ahead. I'm anticipating so many things. I'm anticipating the faithfulness of God to be my mainstay, no matter what I face! I'm anticipating the promise of peace that passes all understanding. I'm anticipating that God is supplying all my needs, as His Word declares. I'm anticipating sharing

Week Two: Anticipation

family joy, friendships, love, miracles, and so many other blessings while I'm alive and living in this earthly temple. I'm anticipating my eternal home in Heaven. I'm anticipating receiving a crown of life. I'm anticipating the joy of endless worship and praise with the angels. I'm anticipating seeing loved ones in Heaven who have already made it there. I'm anticipating seeing the indescribable beauty of Heaven, and seeing Jesus Christ, my Lord and Savior, face to face. I cannot even begin to imagine the wonder of that event, but I am anticipating it. I'm looking forward with excitement and expectation to my eternal home.

Anticipation is a great thing. When I think about my relationship with Jesus Christ, and what I have in Him, I am filled with anticipation. As a Christian, I have a great expectation and great anticipation. It is my hope. My hope is in Christ. My hope is in His Word. My hope is in Him!

Joy for Life

Autumn

I have said for years that fall is my favorite season. I love the colors and the holidays. I love the feel of fall in the air. I love putting out pumpkins, mums, and fall scented candles. It's a wonderful season. Each year about this time, I'm reminded of a special fall memory that I cherish.

Several years ago, Terry and I had the opportunity to travel to the Smoky Mountain Children's Home with a group of ten ministers and wives to be part of the dedication service of a home our churches had helped to build. It was a beautiful home, designed for about ten children, plus two house parents. We were there to give thanks and dedicate the home to God's service. It was truly a memorable time. My heart was really touched by the love that I felt and sensed that day from the children and all the wonderful staff.

It was early October, and we enjoyed the scenery in the lovely Tennessee mountains. I enjoyed seeing many displays of hay bales, pumpkins, mums, and fall décor in many of the yards we drove by. I enjoyed time with our friends, as we had a fun trip together. It was great!

I remember so well that crisp, cool, fall morning when we gathered on the lawn of the home we were there to dedicate. The breeze was gently blowing, and the leaves were falling on the ground where we were standing. It was a quiet, serene morning. Standing there with about 25 others, I could hear the minister that was saying words of gratitude, and would be praying a prayer of dedication. I don't remember his prayer. What I remember is the sound of the leaves in the trees as they were rustling and then falling all around us. The sound of the leaves falling from the tops of the trees, falling through the limbs to the ground, began drowning out the voices of the people speaking a few feet from me. I heard the rustling sound and looked up. I could see a little sunshine through the tall trees, heavy with golden yellow and orange leaves. I began to feel tears roll down my cheeks as I sensed the wonder of God's creation, the beauty of the autumn leaves in those tall trees, and the love He had so abundantly lavished on me. It was a moment that I knew was a gift from God. It was a moment that I knew would be remembered, as I sensed the love of God in a special way. I really don't recall what was said by any person that day. I'm sure it was a lovely prayer of dedication, and sincere words of appreciation for the gift of love that had been given, but I cannot remember even one word or phrase that was shared by people that day. What I do remember is the incredible sense of gratitude and amazement for my loving creator, as I experienced His love, goodness and His beautiful creation on that autumn day. I'm so thankful for the awareness of His presence that day. I'm so thankful for the awareness that His presence is with me every day, just as it was on that beautiful autumn morning.

Entering a new season is yet another gentle reminder of the faithfulness of God in our lives. Some of you face difficulties or struggles. Some have physical, financial, or emotional challenges. Each season brings challenges. But don't forget, each season also brings new wonders. Each season brings new opportunities for God to express His love and faithfulness to you, as you learn to grow in Him and His knowledge, love, and grace. Don't ever feel alone, for He is with you, and He loves you! Look for those opportunities to experience His love in your life. It may be in the rustling of the leaves falling gently on the ground around you. It may be in the hug of a friend, or the smile of a child. It may be in the words of encouragement someone shares with you. It may be in a text or an email. It may be in the words of a Bible verse you read. It may be in the Sunday morning message you hear from your pastor. Just be aware that God expresses His love to you in many ways. Don't miss it!

I don't know about you, but I can't wait to get my pumpkins and mums on the porch. Thank you, Jesus, for your faithfulness.

Joy for Life

Week Four: Bluebonnets

Bluebonnets

It's bluebonnet time in Texas! They have been so beautiful this week. I've enjoyed seeing several beautiful fields of bluebonnets every day during my commute to Dallas.

I pass through one area of town that is not the most desirable area. Parts of it are run down and you are sure to keep your car doors locked. However, sitting at a stop light this week on that unsightly, undesirable stretch of road, I looked across saw a field of beautiful bluebonnets. While I was waiting on the light to turn from red to green, I was staring at a sea of gorgeous blue just a few feet away. I was by myself, but I smiled. I did not even notice the undesirable the rest of the week. Instead, I wanted to see those lovely flowers each day. God has created such beauty for us.

It brings to mind one of my favorite scriptures—I know some of you can quote it by heart.

> Finally, brethren, whatsoever things are true, whatsoever things are honest, whatsoever things are just, whatsoever things are pure, whatsoever things are lovely, whatsoever things are of good report; if there be any virtue, and if there be any praise, think on these things (Philippians 4:8 KJV).

Joy for Life

In life, there will always be things that come our way that are not desirable, just like that not so desirable stretch of highway I drive through every day. In life, there will always be tests, trials, and circumstances that try to bring us down. I know because I've experienced many uninvited trials and circumstances in my own life. In life, there will be stretches of ugly road, with unattractive surroundings, but if we turn and look on the other side of the road, we might just see a field of beauty. We go through trials, but there will always be something to be thankful for. We go through temptations, but there will always be a way to resist the temptation. We go through difficulty, but through Christ, we can find the strength to make it through whatever we face. When we think there is nothing beautiful in the middle of what we are going through, we need to just open our eyes and look around. There is a field of beauty there. It may be in the middle of the undesirable trial. It may be in the middle of an undeserved, difficult circumstance. There is a field of beauty in sight!

As I read this scripture in Philippians, it encourages me to think on the things that are lovely—things that are honest, just, pure, true, and of good report. It's up to me. I choose to think on the undesirable, or I choose to think on the lovely, pure truth. The truth is that God so loved the world that He gave His only Son to die for our sins and offer us eternal life. Whoever chooses Him as their Savior receives that gift of eternal life. The truth is that He created me and He loves me. That is amazing. He created you and loves you too. He is altogether lovely and pure. He is my Savior, and I love and adore Him. He has blessed me beyond measure. Now, this is a good report!

Joy for Life

Week Five: Change of Plans

Change of Plans

When was the last time you had a change of plans? I'm not talking about changing the menu for dinner, or changing your mind about whether or not to go shopping or to the movie. I'm talking about a big change in a big plan. Most of the time, we don't really understand the magnitude of these changes. Many times, we are not aware of all that is happening, but we know things have changed. Plans have changed. There is a definite turn in our road of life.

I was thinking recently about some of the turns in our road through the years, and how we do not understand why everything works out as it does. I do know we trust God's direction and His hand in our lives. Just a few evenings ago, I was reminded of a particular event and how God spoke to our hearts in a very special way, giving direction and a change of plans.

It was in our early ministry. My brother, Eddy, and his wife, Leah, were on staff at a church in Ohio. We took a trip to visit them. Our oldest daughter, Michelle, was a toddler, and we were very excited as we loaded the car and took off. We had a wonderful trip with our little girl and enjoyed the journey. We arrived at our destination and had fun visiting with Eddy and Leah. Through a series of events while there, we were offered a very inviting and exciting ministry opportunity at a beautiful church close by. We met with a pastor and church board, and were offered a job as youth and music ministers at the church. It was a dream come true. Terry would be in full-time youth ministry, and I would be involved in the music of this church. We accepted the offer and located an apartment to move into. We met again with the church board before the Sunday evening service, and they gave us a generous check to pay for our moving expenses.

We were introduced as new staff members in the evening service. The three of us were brought to the stage. Terry greeted the congregation and I played the piano and sang a special song. It was indeed an exciting time in our life and an exciting plan. As we were seated in the congregation during the remainder of the service, Terry and I both realized that God was guiding us in a different direction. This move to Ohio was not in His plan, even though it sounded so inviting to us. We did not have the opportunity to speak to each other, but during the service Terry slipped a piece of paper to me. I unfolded the paper and he had written, "Are you with me?" I nodded to him. We had not spoken a word to each other, but yet I knew we were on the same page spiritually.

Week Five: Change of Plans

To quickly finish this story, even though we did not have the opportunity to talk with each other, Terry went to the pastor at the end of the service that night. He told him that we appreciated this opportunity, and we did not understand why, but God had let us know this was not His plan for us. He told the pastor he would do both of them a favor, give the check back, and not make this move. We did not understand, but we did know the leading of the Spirit of God in our lives. We made the choice to listen and obey His guidance. If we had made the choice to not obey His guidance in our lives and stay in Ohio, I do not know what the result would've been.

I'm thankful that God gives us direction and He gives us free will to choose His guidance. He gives me the opportunity to follow Him in obedience, or choose to ignore His guidance and go my own way. I want to follow His guidance in my life. I want to be willing to follow Him, even if it means a change in the plan I have, or a turn in the road of my life. I have come to understand that His plans and His ways are the best. He loves me and He loves you, and His plan for us is to bring Him glory with our lives. Above all else, I want to follow His plan and His will.

Are you facing a change in plans? Are you willing to follow His leading, even if it means a turn in the road? If He is leading you, there is no need to fear. If He is leading you, He is making a way for you. He never fails us, and He never makes a mistake. Trust Him. He loves you!

May the God of peace, who through the blood of the eternal covenant brought back from the dead our Lord Jesus, that great Shepherd of the sheep, equip you with everything good for doing His will, and may He work in us what is pleasing to Him, through Jesus Christ, to whom be glory for ever and ever. Amen (Hebrews 13:20-21 NIV).

Week Six: Changes

Changes

Whether we like or dislike change, we are faced with it regularly and consistently. For over nine years, I have worked in a hospital building with a great view of downtown Dallas. Several people have made comments like, "How do you get any work done with this beautiful view?" When I'm still at the office after dark, the magnificent lights of the skyscrapers are quite a sight to see. I've enjoyed my view for over nine years, but recently my office relocated to the other side of the building. Now I see the other side—and the view is mostly a parking garage! I have tried to stay positive and thankful that at least I have a nice office and have two big windows and can still see outdoors.

Change. It comes in many different ways. When it makes us happy, we like it. When we lose a few pounds and our clothing size goes down, we are happy about change. When we get new furniture and change out the old for new, we are happy about it. But some changes come unexpectedly, inconveniently, and are difficult to navigate through. It may be the loss of a job, or an unexpected and sudden

Joy for Life

relocation, requiring a move, selling a house, finding a new home, and changing schools. Change comes when your children get married and leave home, or graduate and move out to go to college. Instead of knowing their schedules, that they're getting good meals and plenty of rest, and that they are home safely each night, change has come and you can't know all the details. Change comes when health issues cause more trips to the doctor, and medical bills begin to require more of the income that you were planning for retirement. A surgery or sickness can cause change in your lifestyle for weeks, months, or even years. And with the hardest change—the loss of a dear, beloved one—life as we have known it forever changes.

I want to encourage you today about changes that have come or are coming to your life. I have taken the word "change" and want you to think of each letter and the following thoughts from God's Word:

C – Courage

H – Hope

A – Acceptance

N – Next

G – Gladness

E – Everlasting

Courage: "This is my command—be strong and courageous! Do not be afraid or discouraged. For the Lord your God is with you wherever you go" (Joshua 1:9).

Hope: "'For I know the plans I have for you,' says the Lord. 'They are plans for good and not for disaster, to give you a future and a hope," (Jeremiah 29:11).

Acceptance: Accept that the past is the past, and you cannot change the past. "…I focus on this one thing: Forgetting the past and looking forward to what lies ahead" (Philippians 3:13).

Next: What's next in your life? "…looking forward to what lies ahead. I press on to reach the end of the race and receive the heavenly prize for which God, through Christ Jesus, is calling us" (Philippians 3:13-14).

Gladness: No matter what is happening in our lives, we worship the Lord who is worthy of our praise. "Worship the Lord with gladness; come before Him with joyful songs" (Psalm 100:2).

Everlasting: No matter what you are facing or what changes have come or will come, our Lord does not grow tired or weary and He is with you. "Do you not know? Have you not heard? The Lord is the everlasting God, the Creator of the ends of the earth. He will not grow tired or weary, and His understanding no one can fathom" (Isaiah 40:28).

Joy for Life

Week Seven: Crayons

Crayons

Crayons and coloring books were some of my mainstays as a child. I especially liked the big sheets of manila construction paper so I could draw my own pictures. I grew up with crayons that were blue, red, brown, yellow, orange, green, purple, and black. Eight simple colors. I always colored the grass green, and had a yellow sun in the corner of the top of the page. Trunks of the trees were brown, and the trees would have either red apples or orange oranges. Flowers could be purple. Of course, the sky was always blue. As I got older, more colors were introduced. We had sky blue or navy blue, and fuchsia or maroon. We had lime green or forest green, and chocolate brown or light brown. I could have flowers that were lemon yellow or carnation pink. Coloring became more complicated, because I could no longer just have a blue sky or green grass. I used different blues for the sky, and blades of grass were multiple shades of green. Creativity would flow as the flowers, trees, and lakes would fill that large, blank page with color.

Coloring on that piece of paper was fun, and it reminds me a little bit of my life. As a kid, with a lot of blank space on that page, it's pretty simple. Choices are not that complicated when you're young and everyone is taking care of you. The sky is blue, the grass is green. Apples are red, and oranges are orange. But as time goes along, more and more choices have to be made. Just like choosing the colors for a masterpiece on the large page of construction paper, we must be careful as we make our choices in life.

The most important choice I ever made was to accept Christ into my heart. The Bible tells us that Jesus gave His life for us, so that we could have eternal life. He gave His life for whosoever believes in Him. I am definitely one of those "whosoevers" He was talking about. That decision, that one choice that I had to personally make to receive Christ, opened the door for Him to begin coloring my life with His creative hand.

I can see how His hand has moved so lovingly as He has walked me through the bluest of blue skies, as well as shielded me through the blazing bright orange colors when I went through the fieriest of trials. He has colored my life with some wonderful walks on the powder soft sands of the ocean, and He has held my hand through the rockiest of river beds when my feet could not stand the sharp edges. My life is truly a work of art—not because of what human eyes can see, but because of the grace of God that has colored every day of my life with His loving touch. I can look in the mirror and see flaws, but He looks inside my heart, and He has colored it with His love. I look at the difficult times of my life and see scars, but He sees a healed wound.

I love the beautiful colors I see everyday. Bluebonnets are such a magnificent blue. The Texas sunrise is incredible. The pinks and oranges are so majestic, I cannot find enough descriptive words to tell about them. I'm surrounded by beauty, but I know that we—you and me—are the handiwork of God. Our lives are His work of art, and we need to do all we can to bring our Artist glory with these lives He created.

> For we are God's masterpiece. He has created us anew in Christ Jesus, so we can do the good things he planned for us long ago (Ephesians 2:10-11).

Joy for Life

WEEK EIGHT

Dancin' Shoes

I had surgery on my foot one October. I was instructed to stay off it for an entire week, and couldn't drive for a considerable amount of time. I wore a clumsy, and rather clunky therapeutic contraption on my right foot for six weeks. As you can imagine, my normally busy schedule was rudely interrupted. My activities came to a halt, and I even had to learn how to use my left foot on the piano pedal instead of the right foot. On a positive note, I enjoyed some recliner time for a week, read some books, and enjoyed the guests that came by to visit. My mom and dad came over one day and she brought me a book called *Put on Your Dancin' Shoes* by Liz Heaney. Now, keep in mind that I couldn't put on any shoes at that moment (particularly any dancin' shoes), and I didn't read the book immediately. However, I have enjoyed reading it since then. It is an inspirational book of positive quotes and short stories. One of the chapters starts with this quote:

> When we put on our dancin' shoes, we announce our willingness to embrace each moment as a gift from God, bursting with abundant potential.

I love that thought. I love the fact that whether we have on dancin' shoes or not, we can "embrace each moment as a gift from God, bursting with abundant potential."

I've lived some days that I really did not want to embrace. I've experienced some situations that did not strike me as a gift from God. I'm sure you have too. What I have discovered through the years, and what I try to communicate through these devotions, music, and through my words is that God is faithful. Even in the days we don't see potential, or we do not see anything to embrace, God is still faithful. He is there. He is giving us a gift—the present—and it is up to us to embrace the day and find the bursting potential.

What can you embrace today? I encourage you to embrace your loved ones. I encourage you to embrace the hope we have in Christ. I encourage you to embrace the joy of fellowship. I encourage you to embrace God's Word and let it be food for your soul. If you are young, embrace your energy and plans for great things God has for you. If you are not so young, embrace God's goodness to you through your life, and the assurance that He cares for you and knows your every need. If you are super busy, always on the go, with little time to rest, embrace the knowledge that He is always with you, and you never go alone. There is so much to embrace! What potential do you see in your life? God desires to work in you, and He is more interested in you than you can imagine. I'm inspired just thinking about the love of Christ that is real to my life and in my heart.

WEEK NINE

Determination

Are you determined? Being determined reflects being firm and resolute. I've been pretty determined in some aspects of my life. There are times some people might refer to my determination as being strong-willed or even stubborn. (Imagine that!)

I'm determined to do the right thing. I'm determined to be a kind and joyful person. I'm determined to be a great wife, mother, and grandmother. Even though I'm aware that I fall short at times, I am determined to keep trying and keep doing my best to be the best me I can be.

A few years ago, as we entered a new year, I was determined to improve my piano skills. I decided to do this by playing the piano each and every day of that year. That may not sound like such a big deal to some people, but for me it was a major undertaking. I have seen some piano students that practice daily (for example, my grandsons), and I applaud them and their determination and discipline. However, for me, it is a challenge. Since I work in Dallas every day during the week, often have church or other events in

Joy for Life

the evenings, and we have busy weekends, it leaves very little time to dedicate to practice. But I was determined. I made up my mind. It became more challenging as the year progressed. When traveling out of town for my job during the year, I did not know what I would do to play. I shared my dilemma with a friend. Although she was not a musician, she said she had a roll-up keyboard that she would let me borrow. I rolled it up, packed it in my suitcase, and off I went. It didn't sound quite like a baby grand, but it was a piano. I would roll out my piano on the desk in the hotel room and play.

Later in the year, while we traveled out of town with some friends for an overnight stay, I was determined to keep up with the promise I made to play each day. As we traveled, I asked everyone to help locate a music store. Driving through several towns, we never found one. It was getting late. I told everyone in the car that I had to find a piano. I could not rest until I found one to play. We finally realized we were running out of options. There was only one hope for our piano search—Walmart! It was late in the year. I hoped that with Christmas around the corner, the store would have an electronic keyboard of some kind and I could go in and at least play a song or two. It was my only hope and I was determined. Terry parked the car and went into the store with my friend Charlene and me. We were on a mission and it was to find a piano. We went through the aisles, but did not find a keyboard. We finally asked for assistance from a young man that worked in the store. He let us know the only piano they had was a little piano in the toy department. It was just a toy, but it had keys and it played music. I began to play a song. Charlene explained to the store attendant about my determination to play each day of the year. The year was almost over, and I couldn't bear to mess up now. The little toy piano made a plinking sound. I heard Charlene tell the young man who was helping us, "You should hear her play that on a real piano!" It was pretty funny, but I was determined to play that day. My determination paid off. I played every day that year, even if that particular day I only played a toy piano at Walmart.

Being determined to do the right thing for the right reason is a very good ambition. Being determined to be what Christ wants you to be is a magnificent goal. What are you determined to be? What are you determined to do? Are there changes needed in your life to be more Christlike? Are you determined to make the changes necessary to be what Christ wants you to be? Let's be resolute and be firm in our decision to be what Christ wants us to be and do. You will find joy in His will. You will find strength in His guidance.

I encourage you today to be determined in your resolve to serve God. Be firm and resolute in your mind as you move forward in your walk with Christ. "Let this mind be in you which was also in Christ Jesus" (Philippians 2:5).

Let's be determined to be led by the spirit of Christ as we walk through this week.

Joy for Life

WEEK TEN

Do You See the Reflection?

As a minister's wife for over forty years now, I have participated in many wonderful and memorable events with our various church groups. We have accumulated photographs, videos, and memorabilia that capture special moments. One particular event that brings a smile to my face is a women's event that we had a few years ago. It was a lovely event, held at the local country club. While discussing with friends what to wear, we all decided on black dress slacks and lovely tops or sweaters. I went to Dillard's and came home with a beautiful black sweater, sparkling with black and red sequins. I was ready! The special evening came, and I attended the event in style. I was on the stage a portion of the time, speaking to the group, providing some music, and of course, mingling with the crowd, giving hugs and greetings to everyone. It was a great evening of fellowship, food, and fun, just like I had enjoyed so many other times. Many photos were taken, as we smiled and stood with friends. I enjoyed wearing the new outfit so much, I wore it again on Sunday morning to church. As usual, I was up front again during service, and sharing heartfelt greetings and fellowship after the service.

Now, the rest of the story... A couple of days later, the photographs from the country club event were developed. I couldn't believe what I saw in the pictures. After all, I had tried so hard to look nice. I had made sure my hair, makeup, and jewelry were just right. I had purchased a new outfit. While I was there, enjoying the event, everything seemed to be in place, and no one ever noticed. But there it was, glaring in the photographs. Obviously not seen to the naked eye, but so obvious in the photos was a small, clear, shiny strip on the front side of the sweater. I thought "This cannot be..." but I went to the closet, pulled the sweater out, and still there, after wearing it those two times, was the shiny sticky strip on the front, with a line of black letters, **M**. I felt a bit of embarrassment, wondering if anyone had noticed but just didn't want to tell me. I asked a few of my close friends if they noticed it, and they all assured me it was not noticeable or they would've told me.

It does make me think, though. How did that happen? Why did it show up in the photographs? Without getting too technical, I do know that physics teaches that it was simply the flash bouncing back from something reflective in the range of the camera. I did not know there was a shiny strip stuck to my beautiful sweater until I saw the photograph that reflected that bit of refracted light from the reflective strip.

Week Ten: Do You See the Reflection?

Every day, I go to work in Dallas. My hair is styled, my clothes are pressed, and I try to be sure I am fixed. What I've realized is I am not who I want people to see. I want them to see the reflection of someone else. I want them to see the reflection of Christ in my life. Do my attitudes, actions, responses, and behaviors reflect the Christ I serve? Just as a beautiful photograph of a magnificent mountain overlooking a lake shows the reflection of the mountain in the lake, I want my life to reflect the beauty of Christ. I don't think people are going to say, "She sure is Christlike..." But I hope they *will* say, "There's something different about that lady..." or, "There's something special about her...". I want that "something special" to be the reflection of the Light of the World. I want that "something special" to be the reflection of the Bright and Morning Star.

> So all of us who have had that veil removed can see and reflect the glory of the Lord. And the Lord—who is the Spirit—makes us more and more like him as we are changed into his glorious image (2 Corinthians 3:18).
>
> And you yourself must be an example to them by doing good works of every kind. Let everything you do reflect the integrity and seriousness of your teaching. Teach the truth so that your teaching can't be criticized. Then those who oppose us will be ashamed and have nothing bad to say about us (Titus 2:7-8).

Be sure and check all your new clothes for those sticky strips!

Joy for Life

WEEK ELEVEN

Doing Music

Ever since I was a kid, I've loved music. Even before I learned to play piano, I would sing. I had a little record player and some records in my room. I would sing my heart out with "Here Comes Peter Cottontail" and "You Are My Sunshine," As a kid, I remember listening to my mom play piano and organ duets with her kindred spirit friend, Pat. Although I was pre-occupied with coloring books and dolls, I was still listening. When I got a little older and wanted to learn to play the piano, my parents bought an upright piano and placed it in my bedroom. I guess that was the best thing to do for a budding musician, who would take forever to pick out the simplest version of "Twinkle, Twinkle Little Star" from Beginners Book Number One. But, somewhere along the way, the love of music was so instilled that I cannot imagine going a day without singing or playing, or listening and enjoying the beautiful gift of music.

When I was in the second grade, my family lived next door to our small town church. I would get my mom's high heel shoes on, walk across the street, and go to the back of

Joy for Life

the church where there was an old piano for practicing. I would sit on the piano bench with those pretty shoes on, and I would pretend to play and sing for church. I'm sure it was a sight to see and a noise to avoid, but somehow in my heart, I think I was giving God a bit of amusement and joy. I was just a child, and I certainly did not understand all the techniques of how to sing, the dynamics of the piano, or what was expected in the realm of church music. What was certain is that I had a desire to make music, and deep in that little child heart of mine, I wanted it to be something special for God. Some people may think I was just playing church, but I think it was more than playing. It was a prelude of what was to come.

I guess, in one way or another, I've been doing music longer than I've done anything else. I cannot think of a time I have not been involved in church music, and even now, I am still involved each week. I wonder if God is receiving as much joy from the music I do now as He did when I was in the second grade and didn't have a clue what I was doing. There are times we just get so accustomed to doing what we do. During some seasons of our busy adult lives, we lose the childlike passion. I still listen to music all week, I sing and play, I practice. But when I come into His presence, and offer the gift of music that He gave, I wonder, is He still enjoying my gift? I'm bringing my gift to Him, but is the beauty and the melody muffled with the distractions of this life? Is my voice clear and pure, or is my voice just making words and noise, while my heart is not fully engaged in the beauty of worship? Ouch! I think I'm guilty.

I was reminded of these things as I listened to one of our grandsons play in a piano competition. He did an amazing job and I sensed his love for playing the piano. I marveled at his ability to communicate the beautiful music with those fingers of his. This grandmother was beaming with pride. I want to bring that kind of joy and pride to my Father in Heaven. I want Him to see me, His child, doing what I do for Him.

> He put a new song in my mouth, a hymn of praise to our God. Many will see and fear the Lord and put their trust in him (Psalm 40:3 NIV).

Joy for Life

WEEK TWELVE

Don't Miss the Flight!

We love to travel. We have traveled to some beautiful places through the years. Some of our trips have been with family, while others have been with friends. Some of our trips are just special times for Terry and I to enjoy being together. Sometimes it's a pleasure trip, and sometimes it's a business trip. Sometimes we fly, sometimes we drive, and we've even traveled by ship. Wherever we go, and whatever the reason, there is a consistent thread in our travel—we always enjoy the trip. We want to enjoy the scenery and the time for talking and visiting. We want to enjoy food and fun while we travel. Even though the ultimate goal is the destination, it's great to enjoy the trip and what happens along the way.

Some people like predictability and want to plan every stop and event. Some like to just take off without deadlines or schedules, and take as much time as they want to get to the destination. We've traveled all those ways, and each has advantages and disadvantages.

One particular trip we took was to Denver. I spoke at a clinical conference and was so glad that Terry could travel with me. We rented a car and took time to see some sights and enjoy the scenery in the evenings. The last day was a short work day. We decided to go to a popular tourist spot, a candy factory. It was very interesting and fun to watch them make candy, and even get a sample. They had a little ice cream parlor in the gift shop, and we decided to enjoy a treat before leaving. We had plenty of time to return the car and get to the airport for our flight. What we did not count on were some unexpected delays in getting the car back to the rental car location. We began to feel the rush! Significant delays caused us to be late to check in and, to our dismay, we could not board our plane. The plane was still on the ground and had not taken off, but we were not checked in soon enough to board. I asked the attendants at the ticket counter about the next flight that I knew left about an hour later. To my surprise, they had canceled the next flight, the last flight to Dallas that day.

We were placed on the earliest flight, which was to leave at 6:30 the next morning. We chose to make the best of our predicament. We ate dinner at the airport and found a place to rest. We needed to get some sleep, since I was to be back at work the next morning as soon as we got back to Dallas. Terry had noticed the airport chapel earlier in the evening, so we made our way to it. The only other person there was stretched out on the floor sleeping. Terry stayed awake and watched our bags so I could sleep. I made a

Week Twelve: Don't Miss the Flight

little spot as comfortable as I could with a few clothes piled up for a pillow. At 3:00 a.m., a gentleman came in the chapel, stayed at the front for a few minutes, then sat down beside Terry and began to chat. He inquired about our travels. Terry told him what had happened and mentioned that I had to be at work in Dallas the next morning, so I was trying to get some sleep. After some time had passed, the gentleman got up to leave the chapel, reached into his wallet and gave Terry a $20 bill. The gentleman said, "Take your wife to breakfast before you fly back tomorrow morning." I never saw this man because I was sleeping, but I was impacted by his kindness. We had messed up and missed our flight, but he showed kindness to us. Terry and I have often talked about a frustrating mistake on our part being turned into a time of gratitude, as someone showed kindness to us.

Our candy sample and ice cream were good that day in Denver, but the extra few minutes of enjoying it kept us from making the flight. This makes me think about our lives. Sometimes we don't make the best choices. Sometimes we take too much time doing things that do not matter, while missing out on the important things. I'm guilty of it! But just like a kind gentleman had compassion on us early that morning, our Lord always has compassion on us. Don't lose hope, for when we come to Him, He provides mercy and provision. He is kind and compassionate. I want to be more like Christ. What about you?

This I recall to my mind, therefore have I hope. It is of the Lord's mercies that we are not consumed, because his compassions fail not. They are new every morning: great is thy faithfulness (Lamentations 3:21-23 KJV).

WEEK THIRTEEN

Facing Mountains

I have a little book that I enjoy so much. It's called *Children's Letters to God*, compiled by Stuart Hample and Eric Marshall. I've used some of the letters as illustrations on occasion. One that I think is really cute is from a little girl named Joyce. She wrote "Dear God, Thank you for the baby brother, but what I prayed for was a puppy."

I think we have all felt like Joyce at some time. We pray and make our petitions known. When we receive an answer, we may feel like her, *Thanks, Lord, but I think You missed the point of what I really had in mind!*

Maybe it is a health issue: You pray for healing. Instead you receive an unwanted diagnosis, only to find out more treatment is needed.

Maybe it is a job issue: You pray for a better job. Instead you are stuck in a difficult and seemingly dead end situation. (Reminding me of another character, Snoopy, the beloved "Peanuts" cartoon dog. One day he grumbled, "Yesterday

I was a dog. Today I'm a dog. Tomorrow I'll probably be a dog. (Sigh) There's so little hope for advancement!")

Maybe it is a financial crisis: Needs are great. You pray for provision, and it seems that it is scarce, even hopeless.

There are so many other needs and situations I could mention. These things are like a big mountain right in the middle of our road of life. When we face the mountain, we have to do something. We either have to tunnel through it, climb over it, go around it, or just stop moving forward.

I want to encourage you today and let you know that God is listening. He knows exactly where you are. He knows your need and how to meet it. Not only that, He loves you so very much. Keep moving forward toward Him. He is the answer. His answer may not be exactly what we thought it would be, but His answer and provision are the best.

I have faced some mountains in my life. Today I will share a couple of the major ones I have encountered on my journey.

The first mountain I will share goes back, early in our marriage. I was expecting our first child and had many problems through the pregnancy. About four months into this exciting journey of parenthood, I was admitted to the hospital. Through some tests, the doctor determined that I was bleeding internally. He told Terry he had to perform surgery and that there was nothing he could do to save the baby. He went on to say, "Mr. Cross, if I don't do surgery,

Week Thirteen: Facing Mountains

you will not only lose your baby, but you will also lose your wife." I did not even know what was happening. The next thing I remember is waking up in a hospital bed saying, "Is the baby ok?" I was brokenhearted when I found out about our loss. A few days later, the doctor informed us that I probably would not ever be able to have children due to my condition and complications. I am so thankful to God that He answered our prayers and I gave birth to two beautiful daughters! We have always known they both were truly gifts from God.

Another mountain I recall was more recent. Terry was doing just fine, but had to see the doctor and have a common procedure performed. Within 24 hours, he had acquired a sepsis infection. His body was brutally attacked by the infection as he fought hard for four days in the hospital. It all happened so quickly. I did not realize how sick he really was until they began to talk about possible long-term effects, like damage to his lungs and heart. I stayed with him continually, and we know the prayers of family and friends carried us over that mountain. One event that stays with me were the words from one of the night nurses that cared for him (and me!) through the ordeal. She told me one night, "He is so sick. If he had not been as healthy as he was when this happened, we would be having a different outcome." I knew what she meant, as I have heard the stories of others who battled the same kind of infection and have been adversely affected for the rest of their lives. Some even lost their lives. I am very thankful and grateful for full recovery, answered prayers, and God's loving and healing touch for Terry.

He has provided for us so many times and in so many ways through the years. An old song by Oscar C. Eliason comes to mind. It simply says,

> Got any rivers you think are uncrossable? Got any mountains you can't tunnel through? God specializes in things thought impossible; and He can do what no other power can do.

Now that's my God! I love Him so much.

WEEK FOURTEEN

Fishing

Terry and I like to go fishing when we get the opportunity. We are freshwater fishermen. We have a great assortment of artificial lures and different kinds of plastic worms and jigs. We've gone to Bass Pro Shop on occasion and I have found a lure that I want to buy. Terry will sometimes tell me he doesn't know if it's a good lure or not, since it is not known to be great for catching fish. I've told him a few times, "Well, if I was a fish, I would want this one. I love this color. And look how it shines and rattles." Soon maybe we'll get back on the lake and catch some nice ones. We've had a lot of fun on the water and have some pretty exciting stories to tell from some of our fishing adventures.

One of the things we do when we go out is cast the lure out on to the water. *Cast* means to throw or remove something from one place to another. When we go fishing, we take the fishing rod and cast those lures out onto the lake. Sometimes we want to cast far. Sometimes we just cast a shorter distance if it's a likely place to catch a nice bass.

Whenever we go fishing, I enjoy casting. It's a good feeling to throw that lure and see it land in the water. Then it sinks below the surface and disappears from sight. I'm reminded of the scripture where we are told, "Cast all your anxiety upon Him because He cares for you" (1 Peter 5:7 NIV).

Do you have a worry today? Do you have a discouragement? Do you have a disappointment, or something that is troubling your mind? If so, I hope you will focus on taking that worry or disappointment and cast it on Him. Throw and remove it from your shoulders and your mind and do as the scripture says—cast it upon Him, because He cares for you!

Now, here's another thought: When we go fishing and cast out the lure, we always retrieve it. We cast it out, and then reel it back again. However, when we cast our cares upon Him, I'm sure He does not want us to reel them back in. He wants to take them and relieve us of the burden.

I've cast cares on Him many times. What is so incredible and wonderful is that Jesus is always listening. He is always present, and He is always so willing and able to take our burdens and lift our spirits.

Well, I think I'll go and pick out a few lures for my next fishing adventure. Anyone up for a fishing trip?

WEEK FIFTEEN

Have a Blessed Day

A few years ago, I changed my typical parting words from, "Have a great day," to, "Have a blessed day." When I am leaving the cashier at the store, ending a phone call, or wrapping up a conversation, most of the time I say, "Have a blessed day." I am sincere in my wish when I say this. So many times, I perceive that people are tired, discouraged, complacent, or maybe even feel unappreciated. I hope that my sincere and heartfelt statement encourages someone along the way.

I can't imagine anyone being offended by a simple phrase like, "Have a blessed day." I think it is a great thing to say. However, I did hear about a couple of people who lost their jobs for saying it to their customers. I personally think it is unreasonable for anyone to lose their job over blessing someone, but it apparently offended one person to have James, the Walmart greeter in Georgia, wish them a blessed day. Although he had worked there several years, one person's complaint had the management instructing him to stop saying it to the customers. A bank teller in

Kentucky was fired, after 24 years on the job, for wishing someone a blessed day. Hard to believe, isn't it?

I've read various commentaries on Matthew 5 and the meaning of the word *blessed* as it is repeated over and again. I particularly liked the Matthew Henry commentary that indicates that the people who have the eight characteristics listed in the Beatitudes are indeed blessed, meaning they are happy. It is interesting to me that we are happy…if we are poor in spirit. We are happy…if we are hungry and thirsty after righteousness. We are happy…if we are meek. We are happy…if we mourn. We are happy…if we are persecuted and falsely accused. We are happy…if we are pure in heart. We are happy…if we are peacemakers. I encourage you to read Matthew 5 and what the verses say about each of these characteristics and how they help followers of Christ be blessed. I encourage you to read the verses in their entirety to get the full message.

When Terry and I visited Israel, we sat on the hillside believed to be the place where Jesus spoke the words found in Matthew 5. As we sat in the grass on the hillside, a man read the Sermon on the Mount to the group. It was a beautiful experience, as we could envision the crowd on the day Jesus spoke, sitting in the same area where we sat, listening to Him speak these marvelous words.

I will continue to wish people a blessed day. I will continue to leave my New Testament on the top of my desk at work. I will continue to live my life as a testimony of God's goodness. If it offends someone, I choose to let their offense remain their issue, but will not let it become my issue. I will give God praise and thanks every day with my life.

Oh, by the way, James, the Walmart greeter, had such support from the community, the decision to fire him was reversed. I heard that a group even had T-shirts made to wear throughout the community that read, "Have a Blessed Day," to show support for him and his greeting. I applaud people like James and others who take the time to give someone a kind blessing. In this world of political correctness and so much dysfunction, I think it's nice to have someone say, "Have a blessed day!"

So here I go, sincerely and warmly wishing you a truly blessed day—a day full of blessing from our faithful and loving God.

Joy for Life

WEEK SIXTEEN

He Knows My Name

I'm writing this devotion from a lodge in the mountains of Southern California. The stars are incredibly bright in these mountains, and I stand in awe of the majestic work of our creator. The Bible tells me in Psalm 147:4, "He counts the stars and calls them all by name." I don't know how He does it, but I know He does. How can that be? Verse 5 in that passage says, "How great is our Lord! His power is absolute! His understanding is beyond comprehension!" It is truly beyond my comprehension how He can count the stars and even know them by name.

I have an amazing husband, two wonderful, beautiful daughters, two loving sons-in-law, and seven fabulous grandsons. I remember their names. I have an extended family—my precious parents, a great brother and his family, a host of aunts, uncles, and cousins. I remember their names. I have so many friends that I love dearly. I remember their names (at least most of the time!).

When I think about my precious family members, I cannot even imagine that I could or would ever forget

Joy for Life

their names, because they are forever etched in my heart. They are constantly on my mind. Yet, I hear of dear people with Alzheimer's disease who do not remember the names of their loved ones. I'm sure at one time they could never imagine not knowing their sweet wife, husband, son or daughter, or grandchildren; but, somehow, disease causes a lapse of memory that is heartbreaking to everyone involved.

I'm reminded of a time when we pastored a family that had multiple generations in our church. They were a precious family. We had the elderly mother—who we all affectionately called Granny—her older daughter, adult granddaughters, and great-grandchildren as members in our congregation. Granny, in her 90s, became very ill and was hospitalized. She had been losing her memory over the months, and even though she had lived for over 20 years with her adult daughter, it was heartbreaking to see that she did not know who her own daughter was most of the time. We went to the hospital to visit and pray with her. The family tried to prepare us, and let us know that she was hardly remembering or recognizing anyone. As we entered the room, the family leaned over and said, "Granny, you have company. Do you know who this is?" Granny moved her eyes toward us, and much to everyone's surprise said without hesitation, "It's Pastor Cross. I'd know him anywhere!" We all were surprised, and got a heartwarming chuckle out of the event. The family thought it was special that she remembered Pastor Cross, even though she could not remember them.

Week Sixteen: He Knows My Name

As I read the scripture, I see the love of God reflected over and over again. He does not forget his children. I'm so grateful for His amazing love. Scriptures talk of His great love and care for us. He knows all the stars by name; He is aware of the sparrows and the lilies of the fields. He has my name written in the palm of His hand. He is aware of everything about me and about you. He knows our thoughts. He knows our shortcomings and our needs, and He loves us through it all. He is with us in the valleys, on the mountains, in the storm, and in the calm. It's a love like none other. It's a love I never want to be without. Oh, how He loves you and me!

Joy for Life

WEEK SEVENTEEN

Here Comes the Judge

I opened my mailbox last week and had a notice from the County Clerk. The top of the mailer, in large red letters, stated "Official Jury Summons." Yes, I've been called for jury duty once again. I will do my duty and appear before the judge as ordered.

Receiving the notice reminds me of a time I stood before a judge. I was there to contest a ticket I had received. I had recently moved to this little town, and pulled out onto a residential road from a stop sign. I was going a reasonable speed for residential roads, about 30-35 miles per hour. However, I was pulled over by a police officer soon after pulling onto the road. Much to my surprise, I was informed that I was going 35 in a school zone, where the speed limit was only 20 mph. I explained to the officer that I was new to town, and did not know I was in a school zone. But he gave me a ticket, and said I could talk to the judge about it. I realized that I pulled onto the road between the school zone signs, and I felt that it was reasonable to request that I be excused from this ticket. Since I was new to the area, and did not know I had turned from a side street into a school zone. I decided to do just that, and take it up with the judge. I was sure that the judge would be reasonable, and agree with me that I did not deserve this ticket. I felt the judge would agree that it really was not fair to be given a ticket under these circumstances. I just needed to present the facts. I purchased a city map and marked the locations of the school zone signs. I marked the intersection where I had pulled out. I felt that my request was reasonable, and that surely he would see how unfair it was for me to be ordered to pay a fine under those circumstances. I fully expected to receive mercy. After all, I had never received a ticket, and that should count for something, right? I had been a good, law-abiding citizen. I made my appointment to meet with the judge. The day came and I walked into the judge's chamber. I saw the name plaque on the desk, The Honorable Judge Fry. I guess I should have known that with a name like Judge Fry, I was in for a surprise.

You guessed it. Judge Fry did not have mercy. He explained to me that even though I was a new resident, I should be aware of the school zones, and very quickly informed me that I would have to pay the fine. I left extremely disappointed, and knew that I would not be applying for law school to become a lawyer.

In my spiritual life, I need a great deal of mercy. The Bible even says in Romans 3:12, "…there is no one who does good, not even one." None of us are worthy of mercy! The Bible says in Romans 3:23 that all of us have sinned and fall short of the glory of God! All of us—that includes me and that includes you! The Bible also says,

> You were dead because of your sins and because your sinful nature was not yet cut away. Then God made you alive with Christ, for He forgave all our sins. He canceled the record of the charges against us and took it away by nailing it to the cross (Colossians 2:13-14).

That's great, exciting news. It's the Good News. Our sins can be forgiven, and our charges can be canceled. Christ gave His life to cleanse us from our sins, and give us new life. All we must do is repent, accept Him, receive Him into our heart as our Lord and Savior, and start our new life in Him. We can receive mercy and forgiveness for all the sins of the past. No longer are we judged on those sins. Our sins are forgiven. Our past is forgiven. We start a new life, with no charges against us.

I will do my jury duty. While I am there, I will thank God that because of His love for us, I am no longer condemned. I am free! I am forgiven! I hope I never stand before Judge Fry again, but am thankful that one day, I will stand before Judge Jesus.

Joy for Life

WEEK EIGHTEEN

Home

There's an old saying, "Home is where the heart is." Home is such a nice word, isn't it? I enjoy my home. It's a very lovely and comfortable place to live. But when I talk about home, I'm not just talking about our lovely and comfortable house. Home, for us, has been different locations and different dwellings. We've lived in an apartment; we've lived in a duplex; we've lived in a travel trailer. We've lived in a very small house, and we've lived in a spacious house. We've even lived in a house that also served as the church building! What's really wonderful is that they have all been home, because that's where our heart was. That's where we put our feet under the dinner table and had meaningful conversation. It's where we played and worked, laughed and cried together. Home isn't limited to a place or to a dwelling. It's where you and your loved ones are, enjoying life, making memories, and where love is the foundation.

My husband raised pigeons when he was a young teenager. He was fascinated by the birds and their characteristics. We've talked at times about getting a cage, and having

Joy for Life

some pigeons of our own. I was amused a few months back when we went to a flea market and Terry and I went to see the animals that were for sale. He was drawn to the bird cages, and there they were—those beautiful pigeons! He began to tell me about the various breeds that were for sale, and how you could tell from their markings and their characteristics. The lady that was selling the pigeons was quite surprised, and told us that he knew much more about them than she did.

People have been amazed for generations at the ability of homing pigeons to find their way back home. Some scientists and ornithologists that study these wonderful creatures think that pigeons apparently read the positions of the sun and stars in order to orient themselves. Some have thought that maybe it was keen eyesight, since they've determined that pigeons can see and sense polarized light and detect its direction. However, experiments were done where they placed frosted contact lenses on the pigeon's eyes, and yet they still found their way home. Some have said it's because pigeons have such keen hearing, much better than humans, and they can determine location by the sounds from mountain ranges, ocean waves, and thunderstorms. No one knows for sure, but all of this seems so incredible to me. I'm intrigued by the ability of a bird to know when it is not yet home, and the determination that it will not be satisfied until it is finally there.

I sense some of that same feeling. I enjoy my loving, comfortable home here. Yet, deep in my heart, I know I'm

Week Eighteen: Home

not really home yet. It's not because my eyesight is so keen. It's not because my hearing is so sharp. It's not because I have such great sense of direction. (Thankfully, I have a GPS that I depend on for helping me navigate!). It's much deeper than those things. It's because I have treasure. The Bible tells us in Matthew 6:21, "For where your treasure is, there will your heart be also."

Yes, home is where the heart is. My heart is where my treasure is. I've been laying up some treasure, where rust does not corrupt it, and where thieves cannot steal it. My treasure is in Heaven. That's where home is. My treasures will be there—my Redeemer, my family, my loved ones, my friends; laughter, joy, and placing my feet under the table; worshiping my King. I'll have all of this and more, someday, when I get home!

Joy for Life

WEEK NINETEEN

Hot Air Balloon Ride

It was early morning when we parked in that large parking lot and stepped out of our vehicle. The sun was just beginning to rise. It was magnificent weather for our adventure. This was the day that Terry and I were taking a ride like we had never had before—sailing in a hot air balloon! We were excited, and at the same time uncertain of exactly how this was going to turn out. I guess our first anxiety came when we had to sign the consent form stating that they were "not responsible for accidents, up to and including death." But, here we were, and we were going to take a ride. As we watched the operator prepare the beautiful, colorful balloon, we saw the giant wicker-like basket we would be riding in. It was just large enough for five people to comfortably stand. He explained that Terry and I, along with two other people, would stand in the basket with him for the entire flight and enjoy the sights below and in the sky as we sailed for several hours. I asked him where we were actually going to go. He looked at me, smiled, and calmly stated ,"Wherever the wind takes us!"

When we began to rise higher and higher, I was amazed at the serenity that surrounded us. We were literally floating in complete quiet and calm. Occasionally, the operator would have to make a brief noise, as air had to be pushed into the balloon, but it quickly subsided and the atmosphere became still and peaceful once again. The sky was clear, the air was clean, and we sailed. I have seen videos of eagles as they rise up and glide through the sky. I felt like an eagle, rising and gliding. We would see birds flying below or beside us. As we floated over country hillsides, we saw a horse below, heard him shake his head, and saw his mane blow in the wind. We saw a small group of wild pigs and heard them running through the field. It was amazing what we could see, and what we could hear from the heights. We floated over a farm house and waved at the couple standing on their porch below. It was so quiet, we could hear their voices. We called down to them. They answered back and told us to come on down for a cup of coffee. The day and the ride were wonderful. The landing was a little rough, but it was still a most memorable adventure and we are glad we experienced it.

We live in a world of noise that distracts us from every direction. We live in a world full of polluted thinking. I have determined that I will rise above the noise and pollution, and find the peace and serenity that come from one source and one source only. That source is Christ alone. That is where my trust and confidence are found. Isaiah 40:31 is a wonderful Bible verse that says,

But they that wait upon the Lord shall renew their strength; they shall mount up with wings as eagles; they shall run, and not be weary, and they shall walk and not faint.

I also love this verse in the Amplified version:

But those who wait for the Lord {who expect, look for, and hope in Him} will gain new strength and renew their power; They will lift up their wings {and rise up close to God} like eagles {rising toward the sun}; They will run and not become weary, They will walk and not grow tired.

I'm expecting, looking for, and hoping in the Lord. I'm gaining new strength as I rise up close to God. I will enjoy the peace and serenity that is mine in Him. I hope you join me in the journey!

Joy for Life

WEEK TWENTY

Hungry and Thirsty

Are you hungry this evening? I saw a billboard recently that made me want to go have a delicious Mexican food dinner with chips and salsa, guacamole, and enchiladas. And I can't forget the television commercial of the sizzling steak that makes me want to go out for that medium rib-eye. The menu with dessert pictures of chocolate cake with warm filling, and a scoop of ice cream makes me forget any willpower I've had through the week. There is an urge to get something I desire. It seems I never just forget to eat. There are times I do not have time to stop and eat when I want to, but I don't think I've ever come to the end of a day and realized I forgot to eat all day. I will find time to eat, because the desire is there.

That's not all! I also get thirsty. I have to get my flavored iced tea, or go to the drive-in for a cherry limeade or soda. In the summer, when I spend time outdoors, nothing can satisfy me like a drink of cool water to my parched throat. Sometimes, I just have a thirst, and I can't wait to satisfy the desire. I'm drawn to something that will quench that thirst.

When I partake of what I hunger and thirst for, I enjoy it. Drinking that delicious mango iced tea is refreshing. Eating that sizzling, mouth-watering steak is so enjoyable. That salsa and Mexican food help warm me on a cold night. I know I have to have food and water to survive. They are basic necessities of life.

I love the way Jesus gave us word pictures to get His message across to us. When He said in Matthew 5:6 (NIV), "Blessed are those who *hunger and thirst* for righteousness, for they will be filled." I think He knew we could understand what He was talking about. I get hungry and thirsty every day. What He wants me to do is be hungry and thirsty for Him, and the wonderful, amazing, incredible, satisfying, indescribable relationship with Him that will fulfill a hunger and thirst within us like nothing else can. I should hunger and thirst after Christ, as He satisfies the desire that can only be filled by the relationship I have with Him. My relationship with Christ is my most important relationship. He is the center of my heart, my thoughts, my marriage, my family, my life. Without Him at the center of my life, the hunger and thirst is never satisfied. Oh, I may have a good steak and cool water that satisfy my physical hunger and thirst for a few hours, but only Christ can satisfy the hunger and thirst deep within. He once told a thirsty woman who was drawing water from a well "…whosoever drinketh of the water that I shall give him shall never thirst" (John 4:14 KJV).

Week Twenty: Hungry and Thirsty

Are you hungry and thirsty for a deeper, more meaningful relationship with Christ? I am! I cannot wait to spend time with Him and enjoy His presence and His love. I want to serve Him and be more like Him. I want to draw near to Him and learn from Him. My hunger and my thirst can be filled. Yours can too!

Joy for Life

WEEK TWENTY-ONE

Hunting

I prepared dinner this evening with venison from a deer harvested last year by my husband, Terry. Last week I said to someone, "My husband is a hunter." He said perhaps I should've said instead, "My husband goes hunting," since he has not harvested meat this year. He does enjoy hunting, and I think I would enjoy going along with him, should time permit someday. It is interesting to me to learn about the science of the hunt, the characteristics of a successful hunting season, and the hindrances of the season.

One thing that I've learned from my hunter husband is that deer possess keen senses. Research has shown that a deer can catch the scent of a human about a half-mile away, and they can also see and hear better than we do. I was particularly intrigued about one study that indicated that deer can't always be fooled by these special deer sprays that are designed to lure the deer to you. Because their sense of smell is so keen, they often determine what is fake and what is real.

Do we do the same with our lives? Do we know what's genuine and what's fake? There are things happening around us continually that seem to confuse people and undermine the truth of God's Word. We must dedicate ourselves to know His Word, so we will not be fooled by the counterfeits and the fake or phony ideas of the world. We must not be led astray into false doctrine or false teachings that do not line up with God's Holy Word. Do we know His Word well enough to sniff out the things that do not totally line up with it? I pray we will know it and know when something is not right.

"Thy word have I hid in mine heart, that I might not sin against thee" (Psalm 119:11 KJV).

In the New American Standard Bible, that verse reads, "Your word I have treasured in my heart, that I may not sin against You."

God's Word truly is a treasure. His Word is what will keep us on the right path, and give us strength for the daily journey. There is nothing that can take the place of the Word of God.

WEEK TWENTY-TWO

Hurricanes

Terry and I lived in the coastal area of Texas for several years. I loved the tropical climate and the beautiful, lush green grass. I loved the tropical plants, flowers, and palm trees. It was great living on the coast, but one negative thing was hurricanes.

We went through hurricane season each year. A key word here is season. Hurricanes and storms didn't happen the entire year. They were just a threat during the season. Like the hurricanes and tropical storms, the trials and storms of our lives come for a season. They will not last forever. They will not continue on and on. They last only for a season and then they are gone—until another storm season rolls around. After the storm season is over, and the storm has passed, there is a time of reforming, rebuilding, and renewing of what has been damaged. Damage comes, but a time of rebuilding takes place, and things are repaired. The season of storm passes, and a season of productivity returns.

Another thing about a hurricane that I remember so clearly is the fierce wind that blows. I recall a time we saw the wind blow so hard, it literally picked up a storage building from a nearby yard, and it went tumbling down the road, end over end, like a toy. It was a frightening experience. The winds blew so hard that the big palm trees which stood so tall would begin to bend. As the wind blew stronger and stronger, the palm trees would bend farther and farther.

The palm trees are quite amazing, though. They will bend, and they will bend farther, and keep bending—but they do not break! Their strong roots keep them in one piece. When the storm is over, they will rise up again, strong and tall.

I want to remind you that storms will come to every one of us. No one is exempt from storms. Rich and poor, young and old, male or female—we all face storms at some time. Storms come in many different ways. You may be facing a financial storm. You may be facing a storm in your spiritual walk, in your health, in a relationship, or a career or school situation. I want to encourage you today to be like the palm tree. When the storms come, be sure your roots are deep in God's Word. The fierce winds will blow and you may become injured. You may feel that you are bending until you will break. But like the palm tree, you can survive the winds and the storm. Receive courage today and know that you will rise up after the storm and be strong again.

"The godly will flourish like palm trees" (Psalm 92:12).

WEEK TWENTY-THREE

I Gained an Hour

We're instructed to set our clocks back one hour each fall. Some people say, "We gained an hour!" Now, I don't think we really *gain* an hour. In reality, we have the same number of hours as we had before we set our clock back, we just get the sense of gaining an hour. If I forget to set my clock back, I still have the same amount of hours, don't I? I will be traveling to California next month. I "gain" two hours every time I go there. Of course, when I fly back to Texas a couple of days later, I will "lose" two hours! I know I cannot reclaim the same two hours I lost when traveling, but yet, we talk about those hours in terms of losing or gaining them.

What are we doing with our time? We worship, enjoy our family, sing, work, eat, sleep, plan, travel, and play. We meet people, help people, and love people. We read, write, pray, learn, and grow. We do so many wonderful things! But then there are days we worry, stress, resist, fret, and forget that God is with us and for us. There are days we forget to praise Him because we are fearfully and wonderfully made.

There may even be days we forget to thank Him for the beautiful gift of life He has given us.

There are times of triumph for all of us. We should remember the Scripture that says,

> The Lord shall preserve thy going out and thy coming in *from this time forth*, and even for evermore (Psalm 121:8 KJV).

He is truly with us in the time of victory and He keeps us in our going out and coming in. There are also times of trouble for everyone, but another scripture we should remember is,

> For in the *time of trouble* He shall hide me in His pavilion; in the secret of His tabernacle shall He hide me; He shall set me up upon a rock (Psalm 27:5 KJV).

I love the picture I see in this verse. We will all have a time of trouble, but He will hide us in a safe place, and even set us upon a rock. When I'm standing on a rock, my feet are standing firm. When I stand on a rock, I'm not sinking or shifting. When I'm standing on a rock, I feel secure because I'm standing on something solid. In our time of trouble, He hides us and sets us on a rock. I'm standing firm, in days of triumph or in days of trouble. I'm standing firm, not just on a rock, but on the Rock—Christ Jesus!

What about you? When you are facing a time of trouble, the place you need to go is to the Rock. Stand on the Rock, Jesus Christ! He is the Rock on which we can stand and be secure. Even when you are enjoying a time of blessing and victory, keep your feet on that solid rock.

Joy for Life

WEEK TWENTY-FOUR

I Hear Christmas Music

Terry and I were in a home improvement store this week, looking at tools and lights. I began to sing with the music playing over their speakers, and then I said, "Isn't it great to be in a store and hear music playing about the King of Kings and Lord of Lords?" I was joyful just hearing it. Here we are, nearing December, and Christmas music is playing everywhere. I just love it!

I wonder, as we go about this time of the year, how many of us will hear the music playing, recognize familiar tunes and words of the songs, and even sing along with some—but may fail to grasp the message of the carols of Christmas? I want to encourage you to truly hear the messages of each song as we hear about the birth of Christ. He was born of a virgin. His birth was a fulfillment of prophecy. He was born to be the one who came to give Himself as a sacrifice to take away our sins. He truly brings "Joy to the World." As I hear these songs, there are several that refer to "Immanuel," which means, "God with us." I stand in awe of this truth: God—not a God that is far removed from my

Joy for Life

life and my situations, but a God that loves me so much, He is God with me. God with us!

God is with us on Monday, when we go to work and face stress and pressure and need guidance. God is with us on Tuesday, when we go to the doctor, and hear the outcome of lab tests or other conditions and need peace. God is with us on Wednesday, when we feel lonely or discouraged and need a friend and a companion. God is with us on Thursday, when the car won't start, or the washing machine breaks down and we need a provider. God is with us on Friday, when we lose our wallet or car keys and just need someone to assure us that everything will be all right. God is with us on Saturday, when we are sick in body and need a healer. God is with us on Sunday, when we need our loving Father to embrace us and give us grace.

Yes, He is our God who provides guidance. He is the one who speaks peace to our troubled hearts. He is our constant companion, our Redeemer, and our Provider. He is our healer and our Savior.

I cannot be lonely or worried when I have Immanuel—God with me. The King of Kings, the Lord of Lords, the creator of the universe, and the maker of my heart is my Immanuel. He is with me. He is with you. I am His child and I am at peace, because He is my Immanuel. I have hope. I have peace. I have love and I have grace abundant and amazing.

Week Twenty-Four: I Hear Christmas Music

I sincerely hope that you, too, have peace in your heart and life. If there is any doubt in your heart, this is a great time to surrender your life and your will to Him, our loving and wonderful Father. Let Him be your Immanuel. God—With Us—Always!

Joy for Life

Week Twenty-Five

I Remember a Stormy Night

Today is a beautiful day, but every day is not picturesque and sunny. There are days when a storm rolls in and the sun is not to be found. The skies are dark; the atmosphere feels dreary. In those times, it's comforting to know that Jesus is still Lord, just as He is on a sunny day like today.

A few years ago, we lived in Houston. A terrible hurricane hit the area. A large tree fell in our back yard, just outside the bedroom window where our daughters were sleeping. It was frightening for us, although the girls slept right through it. The wind was howling, rain was pouring, and the lightning was flashing. Terry wanted to go make sure everything was all right at the church, and ventured out for the short drive from our home. He came back, very thankful that he made it, and let me know he should not have gone. While he was out, a storage building went tumbling across the road in front of him in the high winds. He could feel the strong winds almost lift the vehicle off the road. That storm lasted a few hours, but the aftermath was much longer. We, along with most of our town, were without electricity for 10 days. We learned how to do what we needed to do during the daylight hours with no electricity, because at night we only had flashlights and candles. Stores quickly sold out of batteries, flashlights, candles, ice, and bread. Since there was no power to keep refrigerators and freezers running, everyone was cooking up their food. We had several neighborhood or church family cook-outs to share what we had all taken out of our freezers. Although we did not have electricity, we had a gas hot water heater and stove. Our gas was still working, and several people that had all electric homes came to use our warm showers through that ordeal. There was a young couple from Georgia who attended our church. They had never been through anything like this hurricane. They stayed in our home until the harshest part of the storm passed over. It was quite an event, as we endured those 10 summer days in Houston without electricity. It was not easy, but we came through the storm.

I guess life is like that in many ways. Everyone experiences sunny and stormy days. Some storms come quickly and others build up for a period of time. But when the storm hits, it usually hits hard. Even a brief storm can leave an aftermath of devastation and confusion. However, through every storm, there is always something good to be found. Good things can be found—like when God's hand provides what we need through the kindness of others. Every storm will eventually end and we see will the sun again. Through it all, Jesus is Lord. He reigns.

Jesus is Lord. I'm comforted by that knowledge. That's all I need to know.

> Don't worry about anything; instead, pray about everything. Tell God what you need, and thank him for all he has done. Then you will experience God's peace, which exceeds anything we can understand. His peace will guard your hearts and minds as you live in Christ Jesus (Philippians 4:6-7).

Joy for Life

WEEK TWENTY-SIX

Inspired

I want to inspire you! According to Miriam-Webster dictionary, inspiration is:

something that makes someone want to do something or that gives someone an idea about what to do or create: a force or influence that inspires someone; a person, place, experience, etc, that makes someone want to do or create something.

When I think about inspiration in my own life, I think about many things. Eating a delicious meal might inspire me to look in my recipe books and cook something wonderful. When I watch or hear amazing singers and musicians, I often feel inspired to reach for more excellence in my own musical endeavors. When I read about someone or see someone doing something benevolent, it inspires me to try to find a way to be more compassionate to others.

In my spiritual life, God's Word inspires me. So many times in my life, as I have heard the Word of God preached, I have been inspired to be a better person. I've been inspired to be a better Christian, wife, mother, friend, neighbor, pastor's wife, and citizen. When I read God's Word and the

Joy for Life

stories of His mighty power in response to great worship, it inspires me to worship.

I want to inspire you to do something new for Christ this week. Step out of the normal. Step out of your comfort zone. Do something different, with the thought in mind that you are doing it for the glory of God. Here are a few ideas:

- If someone expresses a need or difficulty, instead of saying "I'll pray for you," ask, "Can I pray with you right now?" and pray a sincere and simple prayer for them.

- If you hear of a neighbor in need, even if you do not know them well, do something tangible for them. Let them know you just wanted to help out.

- Invite someone to meet for coffee or tea. Tell them you want to thank them for their friendship. Let them know you thank God for them.

   Let your light so shine before others, that they may see your good deeds and glorify your Father in heaven (Matthew 5:16 NIV).

And let us consider one another to provoke unto love and to good works" (Hebrews 10:24 KJV).

WEEK TWENTY-SEVEN

It Was a Crash

It was a Wednesday night, and we had almost arrived at the church for Bible study. We realized we left our stack of study books and Bibles at home. We had to go back. Since we were so close to the church, we dropped off our daughter, Janelle, then Terry and I went back home to pick up the things we had to have for the service. It was a trip we had made hundreds of times over the years. We did not know what that "quick trip back home" held for us that Wednesday evening.

To make a very long story brief, we were involved in a serious car accident. A speeding car hit our vehicle broadside, spinning us around and around. We both had injuries and were taken to the hospital by ambulance. We saw clips of the wreckage on the television news the next day. The accident investigator determined that the driver hit us going 67 miles per hour at impact. As I laid on the stretcher while they were treating us, I looked over at our car. I saw that the point of impact was right in the place where our daughter always sat. I was overcome with tears of gratitude at that moment, thanking God that she was at the church, not in the car with us at the time. Two families from our church traveled the same road and stopped when they saw the wreckage and the ambulance. One of the men said he was so frightened when he saw our car, knowing where Janelle always sat. He was relieved when he found out she was not with us. We were treated at the hospital and released to see a physician the next day. When we were wheeled out, the waiting room was filled with people from our church who had come to pray and show support. We were shaken up, but ever so thankful for God's grace.

For months after the accident, I couldn't go through that intersection without a memory of the sound of that crash. I would shudder, just thinking about how it felt to be blacked out and not know what was going to happen next. Eventually the feelings of anxiety and fear diminished, but even now, the memory remains when we travel that road. That's the way it is with so many things in life. We never forget those things that were so difficult to face, but God's grace and faithfulness heal the wounds that they caused.

God is so good to me. He has blessed me in so many ways. I know His abundant blessings. I also know the pain of tragedy and loss. I have faced some harsh tragedies, almost more than I thought I could endure. I want to remind you, dear friends, that God loves you. When we are going through tragedy, He is loving us and walking with us through the most difficult of days. When we go through trials, He is still loving us and helping us navigate through the difficulties. When we are rejoicing in the happiest and most wonderful time of our lives, He is loving us and I think He also laughs and rejoices with us.

I do not always know His plan for me, but I know His plan is good. I do not always know His purpose for everything that happens in my life, but I know He has a purpose. Be encouraged today and know that He loves you so very much. He has a plan and a purpose for you. It is greater than anything we could imagine on our own.

> I thank my God upon every remembrance of you, Always in every prayer of mine for you all making request with joy, For your fellowship in the gospel from the first day until now; Being confident of this very thing, that he which hath begun a good work in you will perform it until the day of Jesus Christ (Philippians 1:3-6 KJV).

Joy for Life

WEEK TWENTY-EIGHT

Make Up Your Mind

I have a hard time making up my mind. Sometimes simple decisions take too long. Do I want ranch or Italian salad dressing? Do I want a chocolate or a strawberry milkshake? Am I going to wear the black sweater or the red sweater? Simple choices like those do not make a lot of difference in the big scheme of things. Every day I make some simple choices that really do not matter a great deal. I also make decisions every day that are very significant. And, my friends, so do you.

I knew someone who made some very poor choices in her personal life. Although she was an attractive young woman, her choices included some sinful and destructive behaviors that caused her to lose her reputation, credibility, and eventually, a very good job. When confronted with these consequences because of her poor choices, she was very upset. In anger and tears, she told me she was so upset that she was going to kill herself. I quickly told her that if she did that, it would be another bad choice and would be the worst of all the ones she had made. I explained to her that she needed to think about her young children, and the

Joy for Life

result of their lives if she made the choice to abandon them by taking her own life. What a terrible choice that would be! I told her that what she needed to do was immediately start making good decisions. Thankfully, she did not kill herself. Although she never really wanted to have much to do with me after that confrontation, I trust that she did listen to my sincere admonition and started making better decisions. I did what I could do, but ultimately, the choice was hers to make.

Some of our decisions throughout the week may not seem so major at the time, but we find out later they are more important than we realize. An encouraging word shared with someone might be just what they need to keep doing the right thing and not give up. The text we send to someone that says, "I'm praying for you," might be just what they need. The scripture that I read in the morning might be just what I will have in my memory to share with someone later in the day. The way I treat others today is important for my influence with them next week. Things that seem insignificant are often the things that become significant in our lives. I want to remember this concept as I go about my life. Making choices that make a difference should just become natural. We should think about it like we think about the air we breathe. We need to keep breathing to live, but we don't think about it every time we do it. We just breathe. Even though it is a big deal, we don't always think about it as such a big deal. I don't go around wondering if I'm going to breathe. That's what I want to

Week Twenty-Eight: Make Up Your Mind

do with my life choices. I want it to be so natural to do the right thing that I just do it. I don't go around wondering if I'm going to make a good choice.

We are all faced with choices. The most important choice ever is the choice we make to either accept and serve Christ or reject Him. We must decide for ourselves. The Bible tells us how to make that decision. It tells us we are all sinners until we make the choice for ourselves to make Jesus Christ the Lord of our own hearts and lives.

> For all have sinned, and come short of the glory of God (Romans 3:23 KJV).
>
> For the wages of sin is death, but the free gift of God is eternal life through Christ Jesus our Lord (Romans 6:23).
>
> But God showed his great love for us by sending Christ to die for us while we were still sinners (Romans 5:8).
>
> If you confess with your mouth that Jesus is Lord and believe in your heart that God raised him from the dead, you will be saved (Romans 10:9).
>
> ...Choose for yourselves this day whom you will serve... (Joshua 24:15 NIV).

By the way, next time you're faced with either chocolate or strawberry, pick chocolate. You can never go wrong with chocolate.

Joy for Life

WEEK TWENTY-NINE

My Broken Arm

I'm blessed. Right now as I write, I'm in pain. But I'm blessed. Earlier today, I was heading out the door with a small trash bag and a pair of scissors to trim dead leaves from one of my plants. I tripped and fell on a tile floor. The pain was severe and I could not get relief. Terry took me to the emergency room. After all was said and done, I have a broken arm. As I sit this evening, typing with one hand instead of two, I thank God for the many blessings I see in the midst of the pain and extreme inconvenience.

I thank God that the scissors went flying across the floor and did not lodge in my body or on my face. I thank God that as I came tumbling down I did not hit the sharp corners of the table that was very close. I thank God that I was not here alone, because I could not get up without help. I thank God that Terry quickly got me to the emergency room. I thank God that I was immediately taken into a room for treatment with no delay. I thank God that our daughter was here visiting, prepared a wonderful dinner for us, and helped out in so many ways. I thank God that after the x-rays, the initial evaluation was that it is

Joy for Life

a clean break and surgery will not be needed. I thank God for all the friends and family who prayed for and checked on me. I'm thankful for a young grandson who lovingly painted my toenails, since they got chipped during the fall. I'm thankful that there are strong pain medications to help relieve extreme pain. I thank God that He is healing the fracture. I have so much to be thankful for. I am grateful. Yes, I am in pain and greatly inconvenienced, but it is only for six weeks. I am blessed.

As we sat in the room today waiting on x-rays, I made a comment about all the things I needed to do. I told Terry I needed to write my devotion. He quickly replied, "I bet I know what it will be about tonight!" I wasn't sure if I would write about it or not, but I decided to share the experience. Although I'm in pain, God is still so good and He is worthy of and He will receive my worship. I'm still full of joy and great anticipation.

> O give thanks unto the Lord; for he is good: for his mercy endureth for ever. O give thanks unto the God of gods: for his mercy endureth for ever. O give thanks to the Lord of lords: for his mercy endureth for ever (Psalm 136:1-3 KJV).

WEEK THIRTY

My Life is a Book

I enjoy reading. I remember when I was just a little girl, I liked reading a variety of things. I enjoyed mystery stories. I especially appreciated the fun and entertaining books that told about adventures of kids my age. I even remember placing the newspaper on the floor, spreading it out, leaning over, and reading it often. I guess I was quite curious.

When I was about to enter the fourth grade, my dad accepted a pastorate in Brownfield, Texas. The home we lived in was not too far from the public library. In fact, it was close enough that I could walk to the library alone. I became a frequent visitor. There was a pleasant lady that sat behind the desk at this small, red brick library. She kept candy on her desk. I've always loved candy; looking back, I think her offering to share from her dish probably kept me coming back.

These days, it seems much of my reading is for study or preparing for church or work events. In addition to study books, I still enjoy reading a great Christian-themed novel,

Joy for Life

and dearly love reading biographies of people that I admire. I always liked having a real book—you know, the kind you hold and have to turn the page. I didn't think I would want an electronic reader, because I wouldn't have a physical book to hold. However, in recent months, I've enjoyed the Kindle reader on my tablet. I've found a new way to enjoy reading. Even when the lights are out, I can read from my reader.

As I think about the pleasure I receive from books, I think about how my life is a book. There are many people reading this book of my life. What are they seeing on the pages? Are they reading stress and discontent, or are they reading peace and joy? Are they reading pages of fear and doubt, or are they reading pages that reflect trust? Are they reading obedience to Christ, or will they see rebellion on the pages of my life?

What I see, is that on every page, God has been faithful. On every page of fun adventures, God has been there, enjoying the fun. On the pages of worship, He has been there, loving and embracing me. On every page of tragedy and distress, God has been there, the comfort and strength that I needed. On pages when I feel alone, I am not alone, because on every page of this book, God has been my constant companion. On the pages that really make no sense at all, God is somehow bringing together a perfect story that will one day make sense. I want to be a really good book, a book that reflects Jesus on every page. When someone reads my story, from the first chapter to the last, I pray that Jesus is glorified.

> And he hath put a new song in my mouth, even praise unto our God: many shall see it, and fear, and shall trust in the Lord (Psalm 40:3 KJV).

Thank you, Lord, for being on every page of my life.

Joy for Life

WEEK THIRTY-ONE

Never Alone

Did you know that you are never alone? We may feel alone sometimes but we aren't. I love Psalm 42:8 (NIV), "By day the Lord directs his love, at night his song is with me—a prayer to the God of my life." It is wonderful to know that every day, the Lord's love is with me, and at night His song is in my heart.

Yet, sometimes we do not recognize His nearness and His constant presence in our lives. The very next verse, verse 9, of this Scripture reads "I say to God my Rock, 'Why have you forgotten me? Why must I go about mourning, oppressed by the enemy?'" Have you every felt that way—*God, why have you forgotten me?*

I guess we all experience those moments when we wonder if God has forgotten where we are and what we are going through. But He never forgets us. He knows right where we are and the very thoughts we are thinking. He knows the joy and the happiness we're experiencing. He knows the sadness or pain we may be feeling. He knows, He cares, and He is with us both day and night.

I am comforted by the knowledge that God is my constant companion. I have a wonderful husband, but he cannot be with me every moment. I have two precious daughters that I dearly love, and every day my heart longs to see them, but they live too far away for me to see them as often as I would like. My sons-in-law and seven grandsons are so dear and near to my heart, but I cannot be with them every day. I have many other family members and dear friends that I love and would love to be with, but I go months, and sometimes even years, without the opportunity to share conversation and be present together. But my Lord is with me constantly, and I can talk to Him anytime, day or night. And let me tell you, I do just that. I talk to Him throughout the day. I share my thoughts with Him. I share my burdens, concerns, and requests. I praise Him for who He is and for what He has done. I praise Him for being my everything. I worship Him because He is worthy of it. I can talk to Jesus. He is listening. He is concerned about my needs. He is faithful!

I am comforted to know that God is not only present with me at all times, but He is working for my good. We do not always understand what He is allowing, or what He is preparing us for, but we can be assured that He is with us through it all.

I'm reminded of Corrie Ten Boom, who wrote *The Hiding Place*. I read the book, and I saw the movie that was based on it. Corrie and her family were Dutch Christians who assisted in hiding many Jews during World War II.

Their story is intense, emotional, and inspiring. They were imprisoned for their acts of kindness in saving many Jews from the Holocaust. Corrie and her sister were placed in a Nazi concentration camp. The circumstances were gruesome and extremely harsh. As her sister was dying in the concentration camp, she told Corrie, "There is no pit so deep that He (God) is not deeper still."

Corrie Ten Boom stated, "Every experience God gives us, every person He puts into our lives, is the perfect preparation for the future that only He can see."

I agree with Corrie. God sees the future; He sees the master plan of our lives. We may not always sense His presence with us, but He is there. We may not understand the things He allows in our lives, but He is there with us, day and night, giving us strength and comfort.

Joy for Life

WEEK THIRTY-TWO

Noise

I hear so much noise around me, I think I forget to really listen. As soon as I get out of bed, the noise starts. Water faucets, hair dryers, ice makers, dishwashers. Garage door openers, car engine, radio music, news, weather, and traffic reports during the morning commute. Noise. City buses, school buses, work traffic, sirens, trucks, and motorcycles. There is just so much noise. I'm hearing a lot of noise, but what am I really listening to?

For years, Terry and I have enjoyed living in a country setting. One thing we enjoy about being outside of the urban area is having a little bit of wildlife in our yard. We frequently have rabbits, squirrels, roadrunners, crows, and armadillos visit our yard. We've seen coyotes, and even a bobcat on one occasion. One of the things we really enjoy is having bird feeders close to our window so we can see the beautiful birds that come to feast on the seed we provide. I love to watch them, and can identify several by their colors and shapes. I hear them chirping and making beautiful music, but I cannot always identify their unique sound. I have not really listened enough to do that.

I recently heard about an organization for blind people to go birding. While many people think of bird watching, these people are bird listening. They have found great pleasure in identifying the various birds, not by their colors, shapes, and behavior, but only by their sound. I found that so fascinating! In fact, I read about a group of bird watchers and listeners who went birding together. The blind participants heard and identified more birds than those who had eyesight to see the birds. The participants who could not see were really listening! They were not dependent on seeing—they were only dependent on listening.

In our lives, when we need direction or provision, we so often depend on what we see. I think there are times God has already given us the answer, but we are so busy trying to see it that we do not listen for His voice to speak to us. I've been guilty of saying, "I don't see how this can work," when I should rise up with faith and say, "God's Word says that He is able." I should not depend on what I see, when I need to be listening for His Word and what He has said.

I'm reminded of the scripture, 1 Kings 19:11-13 that talks about Elijah. Read it with me: "'Go and stand before me on the mountain,' the Lord told him. And as Elijah stood there, the Lord passed by, and a mighty windstorm hit the mountain. It was such a terrible blast that the rocks were torn loose, but the Lord was not in the wind. After the wind there was an earthquake, but the Lord was not in the earthquake. And after the earthquake there was a great fire, but the Lord was not in the fire. And after the fire there was the sound of a gentle whisper. When Elijah heard it, he wrapped his face in his cloak and went out and stood at the entrance of the cave."

Elijah experienced a strong wind that broke rocks from the mountain. He experienced an earthquake. Then he experienced a fire. The scripture says that the Lord was not in the strong wind or the earthquake or the fire. Elijah did not hear the voice of the Lord in all that extreme noise and those extreme events. But when Elijah really listened, he heard a still, small voice. That was the voice of the Lord, but Elijah had to be listening in order to hear it.

God's voice has often come to me in quiet and still ways. What a comfort to hear His voice, and know that He cares for you and for me. Matthew 10:29-31 (NIV) says,

> Are not two sparrows sold for a penny? Yet not one of them will fall to the ground outside your Father's care. And even the very hairs of your head are all numbered. So don't be afraid; you are worth more than many sparrows.

I find it special to see how the Lord chose the sparrow, a bird that was perceived as having little value, to teach a great truth. He was teaching us that in God's eyes, everyone is significant. He is so concerned with every detail of our life. Even the very hairs of your head are all numbered. That's amazing!

I encourage you this week to listen, really listen for the things God would speak to you. It may be through your Bible reading, or through a song you hear. It may be through a message from your pastor or an encouraging word from a friend or family member. Just listen. In the midst of all that loud and often meaningless noise you'll be hearing, take the time to listen to the still, small voice. Stop looking with your eyes, and listen with your heart. It's amazing what you will hear.

WEEK THIRTY-THREE

Perception

I've heard people say things like, "Everything is going my way. I'm so happy!" I've also heard statements like "Everything's going wrong in my life. I am so upset. I am so unhappy!"

Well, I've found out that there is never a time when everything is just perfect, and there is never a time when everything is going wrong. So much of our thinking is based on our perception (defined as "a way of regarding, understanding, or interpreting something; a mental impression."). Our perception is very important as we navigate through life.

For over 14 years, I worked with a clinical research organization in San Antonio that was based in Rockville, Maryland, adjoining Washington, D.C. Through the years, I made quite a few trips to D.C to visit our home office, Bethesda Naval Hospital, and Walter Reed Army Hospital. My hotel reservations were typically made at a nice name brand hotel in Bethesda. But on one particular trip, our company made reservations at a new hotel I had never heard of. It was nice. As I checked out, I complimented the staff. I told them it was my first stay at their facility, that I had never heard of their name before, but I certainly enjoyed my stay. A young man at the reception desk was pleased with my compliment and asked where I was from. When he heard that I was from San Antonio he told me they had opened a new facility in my area. I said, "Oh great! Where is it located?" He said, "El Paso. How far is that from you?" I told him it was 546 miles to El Paso from where I lived. He just stared at me for a moment, and then said, "Oh yeah. Texas is pretty big, isn't it!" You see, he lived where you can be in three different states in a matter of a few minutes. It was hard to perceive a place where two cities in the same state could be over 500 miles apart.

Sometimes my perception gets all messed up, just like that young man thinking there was a new facility in my area. There are times when I think that what I'm doing is not really making a difference, simply because I cannot see all the results. I do not always perceive that God is guiding me through every day and through every decision. I do not always perceive His presence, even though I know He is with me every moment of every day. I do not always have an accurate perception of the way things really are, because I don't see the whole picture. I only see in my area. My perception is often limited to what I see or what I hear; what I learn or what I know. I realize that God is working in so many ways I do not see, I do not hear, I have not learned, and I do not know. That is amazing, isn't it? The

Bible tells us in Isaiah 55:9,

> For as the heavens are higher than the earth, so are my ways higher than your ways and my thoughts higher than your thoughts.

I'm so glad I serve a God whose ways are higher than mine. He is working, even now, in my life. He is guiding and directing me. He is using me in ways I do not perceive. I believe He is also using you—often in ways you may not perceive. God's word says in Isaiah 43:19,

> See, I am doing a new thing! Now it springs up; do you not perceive it? I am making a way in the desert and streams in the wasteland (NIV).

Trust Him as He leads you and guides you.

Joy for Life

WEEK THIRTY-FOUR

Planting Seeds

As I'm sitting at the desk in our office, I hear thunder and rain falling outside the window. I opened the blinds so I could see the rain and the beautiful outdoors. I'm thankful for the rain because a few weeks ago, I planted some flowers in our shrub bed. As I planted the flowers, I talked to them and told them that I wanted them to grow tall in the sunshine, have beautiful flowers, and stay healthy. (Yes, you did read that correctly. I said I talked to the plants while I was planting them, and no, I'm *not* crazy. I just do things like that sometimes.) As of now, all the flowers are thriving, so talking to them evidently didn't harm anything.

As I think about the plants I planted in the shrub bed, I think of my own life. What seeds have been planted in my heart? How have they grown? I also think of seeds I have planted in the heart of someone else. What kind of seeds have I planted in my family, friends, and professional colleagues? I want to plant good seeds in these relationships and in these hearts. How can I plant good seeds?

Finally, brethren, whatsoever things are just, whatsoever

things are honest, whatsoever things are just, whatsoever things are pure, whatsoever things are lovely, whatsoever things are of good report; if there be any virtue, and if there be any praise, think on these things (Philippians 4:8 KJV).

We must plant whatever is true, honest, just, pure, lovely, good, and virtuous. The law of nature, as well as the Bible, teaches us that whatever is planted is what will grow! "Don't be misled—you cannot mock the justice of God. You will always harvest what you plant" (Galatians 6:7).

As a mother, wife, and woman of God, I want to plant pure, lovely, righteous, and virtuous seeds. I want to see these characteristics grow in the soil of all those I have touched. In my own heart, I want to continue to plant the good seed and see a good harvest of love and righteousness. It is important to keep the soil of our hearts prepared. Keep planting the good seeds, and we will see the good harvest.

As I reflect on these things, one of the most beautiful and rewarding results of seed planting is seeing the two beautiful daughters God blessed us with, as they have grown into wonderful women filled with the spirit of God. Their lives are such a great blessing! Good seeds were planted in their hearts, and now they are planting seeds of faith and righteousness in the lives of their own families and friends.

Keep planting good seeds. You will see results!

Procrastination

Don't ask me why, but all week I've felt that this devotion would be about procrastination. I kept thinking I would sit down and write it, but something else would come up and I would postpone the task. I kept putting it off. Oh my! I was procrastinating. Why do I tend to do that? Perhaps you are one of those people who never delays or never puts things off. If you are, I sincerely applaud you and think you are in an elite group.

Some people are young parents with children; some are older adults who live alone. Some work at high stress jobs; some are retired and enjoy more down time than they once did. Some are caregivers, students, sales people, or teachers. Whoever you are, I know you are busy. We all have so many things that call for our attention.

I do not intend to procrastinate; it just happens. I make many grand plans of things to complete, but somewhere along the way, I become distracted with some other task. There are times an unavoidable event interrupts the

Joy for Life

schedule. Sometimes I just get tired, and decide to wait until another day.

There are some things we all know we should not put off—check-ups, dental visits, and health screenings. We should pay our bills on time and take care of business; keep the oil changed and air in the tires. Then there are some things that don't get done as planned, and it makes little difference. No one knows except us.

I stopped by to remind you that there is one thing that we should never delay. There is a need in our lives for a savior. Jesus Christ is the Savior we need. In the Bible we read,

> For he says, In the time of my favor I heard you, and in the day of salvation I helped you. I tell you, now is the time of God's favor, now is the day of salvation (2 Corinthians 6:2 NIV).

I'm so thankful that I made a decision to receive salvation through faith in Jesus Christ. There is only one way to receive salvation, none other than Christ. If you have never made that decision, and if you have not prayed that prayer of repentance and invitation for Christ to be your Savior, please do not procrastinate. Now is the time. Today is the day. It's one thing that will make a difference, now and for eternity.

WEEK THIRTY-SIX

Rejoice!

I am drawn to one of Paul's letters, where he wrote to the Christians at Philippi. In Philippians 4:4-7 he wrote to the Christians,

> Rejoice in the Lord always. I will say it again: Rejoice! Let your gentleness be evident to all. The Lord is near. Do not be anxious about anything, but in every situation, by prayer and petition, with thanksgiving, present your requests to God. And the peace of God, which transcends all understanding, will guard your hearts and your minds in Christ Jesus (NIV).

I have heard this scripture many times in my life. We even sing songs written from this passage of Scripture, encouraging us to rejoice in the Lord. When things are going our way, it is so easy to rejoice. But let's look at what Paul says in this writing to the Christians at Philippi. He says to let your gentleness, calm, and confidence be seen by others. Have no anxiety about anything, but in everything, make your requests known to God. Well now, that part is sometimes challenging, isn't it? Rejoicing is easy when there is no anxiety in our life, but not so easy when there is trouble surrounding us.

Joy for Life

Paul himself was writing this letter to his Christian friends in a place that we would not want to be. He was writing from prison. He was in a place where many people would give up hope and be moaning in despair. I'm confident the circumstances were not pleasant at all. Paul was a prisoner, but he writes like a free man. He says to rejoice always—and he even wants to say it again—rejoice! Where does this attitude come from?

I believe Paul had found the secret of living a joyful life. He knew that the peace of God would come through to set guard over his heart and his mind. To me, that indicates that God was bringing peace to his feelings and to his thoughts. Paul was a victorious overcomer, even in the midst of a terrible situation and undesirable circumstances. Paul was at peace. He was even encouraging others to rejoice and to learn the blessing of rejoicing. Paul chose prayer when things were bad and Paul received peace. Paul chose rejoicing over complaining and he received comfort. Paul chose rejoicing, and even though he was in prison, he was living a life of freedom—freedom from fear, anxiety, and depression. He was living a life of joy and peace. I find this so incredibly liberating for my own life. Through rejoicing in the Lord, I can have a life of peace and joy, no matter what comes my way.

I have enjoyed God's blessings this week. He has blessed me with peace, joy, and strength. Yes, I've had some pressures. Yes, I've had some unpleasant circumstances. Yes, I've had some difficulties, just as I'm sure you have.

Week Thirty-Six: Rejoice!

But I'm rejoicing. I have peace. The words to an old song, "Wonderful Peace" by Warren D. Cornell, are in my mind as I write this devotion. The song goes like this:

Peace, peace, wonderful peace,
Coming down from the Father above
Sweep over my spirit forever I pray,
In fathomless billows of love.

He is such a loving and constant friend. I am rejoicing!

Joy for Life

WEEK THIRTY-SEVEN

Restored

Terry and I have a car hobby. We are members of a car club, have some collector cars, and enjoy car shows and events. We've enjoyed making many new friends through our hobby. We even sponsor a car show at our church each year. With our busy schedules, we don't always get to do as many events as we would like to with our cars, but we enjoy it whenever we get the chance. One thing I find interesting in the car club community is the consistent desire of owners to continue investing in the cars. As an example, they may have an absolutely beautiful show car, like a 1957 Chevrolet or a 1969 Chevelle, but it seems they usually have a desire to keep making it better, bringing just a bit more restoration to the car. We talked to a friend at a recent car show, and his 1950s era car looked great, but he had just had some additional chrome added. It seems there is always work being done on these cars either under the hood or to the body to make them even more special and win just one more trophy! It costs, but to the owner, restoration is an investment in something of value.

I love the 23rd Psalm which says "The Lord is my Shepherd…" and, "He restores my soul."

Now, when I think about that kind of restoration—the restoration of my soul—it makes me so thankful that I serve an amazing and loving Heavenly Father. As I serve Him, He is restoring me each day. He is refreshing me, revitalizing me, and recreating my heart and mind. The cost was extremely high for my restoration. The price? Jesus paid with His life, when He died on a cross for my sins. But He willingly paid the price, because He saw me—and He sees you—as something of value to Him. When we live for Him, we are His trophies. I may get a little rust in my heart, or a little scratch or dent in my attitude. Sometimes I need a tune-up in my thinking. There have been times I needed a complete overhaul. My loving shepherd makes the investment and restores me once again, and I'm so grateful that He does.

Just the other day, Terry mentioned the 23rd Psalm in a message, and made note that the writer didn't say, "The Lord is a shepherd," He said, "The Lord is my shepherd!" He's not just a great shepherd, He's my shepherd. I'm so thankful that He is mine and is restoring me to bring glory to Him. He restores my soul.

WEEK THIRTY-EIGHT

Seeing

Sight is such a wonderful gift. Having the ability to see our loved ones with our physical eyes is fantastic. Being able to see the splendor of God's creation is a blessing. The beauty of a gorgeous sunset, a magnificent sunrise, or the vibrant colors of the flowers cannot be described in words. Seeing mountains, trees, and animals is truly a gift. Although I have to wear contacts or glasses in order to really see these things, I am blessed to have sight and enjoy the beauty all around me.

When I find myself in darkness and cannot see, I feel an urgency to get back into the light. When I cannot see where I am going, feelings of anxiety start to creep in. I want to get back into the light, see what is around me, and see what is ahead.

I have had the opportunity to travel by air many times, and I have always been amazed at how the pilot continues to navigate the airplane through darkness, fog, clouds, and even some pretty rough storms. When the pilot of the plane finds himself in fog or in a blind landing, he depends on the plane's ILS, Instrument Landing System, to assist. There are many things involved in making this happen. Transmitters, radars, markers, and instruments are used to guide these giant vehicles back to safety when the human eye cannot clearly see. Somehow, at least in most cases, the plane is guided safely back to the runway and passengers step off the plane with a story to tell.

In my life, I have experienced many days of gorgeous sunrises and sunsets, the beauty of mountain heights, and fields of vibrant wildflowers. I've also experienced some days, weeks, and months of darkness and fog, where I could not clearly see where I was or where I was going. How did I make it through those times? The grace and love of God became the ILS of my life. He was the Instrument Landing System that guided me back to a place of safety and security. When I cannot see, I trust His Word. I know His Word is true. It says to me that He will never leave or forsake me (Hebrews 13:5). It says to me that I should cast my cares on Him, because He cares for me (I Peter 5:7). It says to me that even though I walk through the valley of the shadow of death, He is with me and comforts me (Psalm 23:4). There are so many truths in His Word that I can look to when I need guidance or provision, hope or courage, strength or restoration. I'm thankful that I can see clearly, but I'm so thankful that in the times I cannot see the path clearly, I'm guided by His Word and the truth of God's grace and love in my life.

I encourage you today to be reminded of His love for you. In the times of your life when you cannot clearly see what is happening or what is ahead, find assurance in His Word that nothing is hidden from His eyes. You are still in His view. He knows exactly where you are, and knows the feelings of fear, anxiety, or despair. He knows, He cares, and He is able to guide you to safety and security once again. Enjoy the journey with confidence. Worship and serve Him. Know He is in control.

Joy for Life

WEEK THIRTY-NINE

Starting and Finishing

I am so good at starting projects. I am not so good at completing everything I start. Now, don't get me wrong. I finish some things. And, yes, my intentions are great. I'm certainly not lazy, but I just get busy and have multiple projects going at once. Some get delayed again and again. Between work, church, getting ready for this event and that program, I just get so busy. Is there anyone else out there like me or am I the only one?

I have been using a list system for about 20 years, making a weekly to-do list. For all these years, I faithfully make a pretty lengthy list each week of things I plan to accomplish. There is a space indicated on the list beside each task to insert the date the task is finished. Some tasks I complete and I write in the date. Other tasks I write "C/O" at the line for completion date. That simply means "carry over" and I carry it over to the next week's list. At least that way I don't forget it!

Now my sweet husband, Terry, on the other hand, is a great finisher of tasks. In fact, the church we started and pastored for over 15 years in San Antonio was a great example of his tenacity to see something through to completion. On one occasion a minister friend visited our church. After looking through the building we had just built, he commented "Terry, one thing that really stands out to me is that everything is *finished*. Even the inside of all the closets is finished nicely. Sheetrock, paint, ceilings—all complete, and nothing left unfinished. Usually there are unfinished areas in most churches." He is good at completing things and I'm glad he is.

I am trying to do better at completing what I start. I see some improvement in this area of my life. I am determined to finish a few things soon that have been in "C/O" status for awhile. But one thing I am confident of: There is someone who is continuing to work on me daily, because I'm not finished yet. There is someone who is still making me into the person He wants me to be. There is someone who is lovingly and patiently helping me to improve my daily Christian walk. He is still teaching me and helping me to grow in wisdom and courage. He still takes my hand, guides my life, and gives me grace and strength. I'm not a finished project yet.

That someone is Jesus. Hebrews 12:2 says we are,

Looking unto Jesus, the author and *finisher* of our faith; who for the joy that was set before Him endured the cross, despising the shame, and is set down at the right hand of the throne of God (KJV).

Another favorite Bible verse of mine lets me know that when He starts something, He finishes it.

Philippians 1:6,

> Being confident of this very thing, that He which hath begun a good work in you will perform it until the day of Jesus Christ (KJV).

In fact, I love Philippians 1:4-6,

> Always in every prayer of mine for you all making request with joy, For your fellowship in the gospel from the first day until now; Being confident of this very thing, that He which hath begun a good work in you will perform it until the day of Jesus Christ (KJV).

I'm confident that God is working in all of our lives. He is everything to me!

Joy for Life

WEEK FORTY

Stormy Days and My Nose

Sunshine and rain. Strong, stormy winds or nice, calm breezes. Bitter cold or cozy warm. We get it all, don't we? No matter who we are, where we live, how young or how old we are, we face it all. My office is on the sixth floor of a hospital building in downtown Dallas. It has two very large windows with a lovely view. Earlier this week, it was cold, rainy, and dreary. Each day, as I came into my office, I felt a chill all through the day. I couldn't seem to warm up. Later in the week, the sunshine came out for a couple of days. The thermostat was not changed, but the office was warmer and much more cheerful, just having the sun shine through those two big windows. I actually felt more cheerful. In fact, it seemed the atmosphere of the entire office changed with a little sunshine coming through! We all love to feel warm, cozy, and calm. We don't like the cold wind or the storms that bring rain. We know rain is needed, and the seasons are necessary, but we still do not like the bitter cold and the storms that come. I'm so glad that even when it's raining on our parade, or when we're shivering in the cold, we can sense the warmth and safety of our Heavenly Father's love. He is our constant, never-absent, but forever-present Father.

We all need to be reminded of that constant presence of our Heavenly Father. One of those times came for me when a surgeon told me I had a skin cancer on my nose that needed to be removed. He sensed my hesitation about letting him cut on my face. He informed me that he could sense my reservation, but that if I waited another year, it would be my entire nose, not just this spot. I explained to him that I knew it needed to be done, and there would be no hesitation if it was on my arm or somewhere else I could cover up. I explained to him "But it's my face. I have to meet with people every day. You're talking about my *face*!" I went in for the surgery and came home with two black eyes, 26 stitches, and a bandage on my face that felt as big as a salad bowl. I was swollen and bruised for a couple of weeks, but eventually I began to hear things like, "You can't even tell it was there!" I knew it was better when one of my young grandsons said, "Grandma, your nose doesn't look as bad as it did!" Now, even I forget about it sometimes until I notice the small scar that remains.

That's the way it is with the stormy days of our lives. They may be painful, but with God's help, we get through them. Then we look back and realize we've made it through that storm. We may still have a scar, but we've come through the trial. Our deep wounds heal. Even though a scar may remain, we are once again whole and complete.

If you are facing a storm, don't give up and don't give in to discouragement. Sometimes we may feel like things aren't getting better, but remember, healing takes time. God's Word tells us, "Weeping may last through night, but joy comes with the morning" (Psalm 30:5). It also tells us in 1 Peter 1:6-7,

> So be truly glad. There is wonderful joy ahead, even though you have to endure many trials for a little while. These trials will show that your faith is genuine. It is being tested as fire tests and purifies gold—though your faith is far more precious than mere gold. So when your faith remains strong through many trials, it will bring you much praise and glory and honor on the day when Jesus Christ is revealed to the whole world.

You will come through the trials. You will experience joy once again. Our Heavenly Father is with us. Endure the trials, but experience His presence. Embrace His love and enjoy His power in your life. He loves you!

Joy for Life

Week Forty-One

Strong Bones

For many years now, I have worked in healthcare research. One topic that seems to have a great deal of interest in our society is bone health. You will hear advertisements and read brochures and magazine articles about the importance of building strength in your bones. Particularly as people grow older, the need to have strong bones becomes more and more evident. Problems with weak bones can be harmful. One problem from this issue surfaces when someone trips and falls, because they are likely to break weak and brittle bones. It's important to take care of them.

Bone marrow is important also. The marrow is a soft, fatty substance in the cavities of the bones, where blood cells are produced. Good marrow helps with strength and vitality.

We want to maintain good physical health in our bones and marrow. We will take calcium. We will take vitamin D. We will eat our vegetables and dairy products in order to keep our bones strong. But what about our spiritual bones? What are we doing to build our spiritual strength? What happens when we trip and fall in our spiritual life? Do we break easily, because our spiritual bones are weak? When faced with a temptation, do we just crumble under a little pressure, or do we stand strong? When we fall, do we have the strength to get up, shake it off, and keep moving forward? Or do we fall, and in a shattered state, just crawl along like someone with broken bones?

One of the great passages in the Bible talks about this subject. Proverbs 3:5-8 says,

> Trust in the Lord with all your heart and lean not on your own understanding; in all your ways submit to him, and he will make your paths straight. Do not be wise in your own eyes; fear the Lord and shun evil. This will bring health to your body and nourishment to your bones (NIV).

What I see in these verses is that I can have strong spiritual bones. Look at each verse and see the instruction that is written, and the result of following those directions. Trusting Him, acknowledging Him in everything in my life, allowing Him to direct my paths, fearing the Lord, and departing from evil will bring nourishment to my bones.

Another wonderful verse says, "Gracious words are a honeycomb, sweet to the soul and healing to the bones," (Proverbs 16:24 NIV). It reminds us that words are so important. The words you say and the things you express can be health to the bones.

I cannot talk about this without mentioning Proverbs 17:22, which tells us, "A cheerful heart is good medicine, but a crushed spirit dries up the bones" (NIV). There are times that I've had a broken spirit, and I know the feeling of weakness that accompanies. When your spirit is broken, there is a helpless feeling that handicaps you from standing strong or moving forward. A broken spirit paralyzes you.

I want to encourage you to build your spiritual bones. Put in practice what Proverbs 3:5-8 instructs us to do. Speak pleasant words, bringing health to our bones.

I will close with one of my favorite verses, Isaiah 58:11. What a terrific promise it is to us, as we read,

> And the Lord shall guide thee continually, and satisfy thy soul in drought, and make fat thy bones: and thou shalt be like a watered garden, and like a spring of water, whose waters fail not (KJV).

Joy for Life

Week Forty-Two

Symphony

We were once given symphony tickets to see Handel's Messiah at the magnificent Meyerson Symphony Center in Dallas. What a fabulous gift! The day came for the event. We dressed in our finest evening wear, arrived at the beautiful auditorium, and made our way to our seats. We were amazed at the architecture and the beauty of the structure.

As the music began, I was absolutely enthralled at the performance. Each musician played with outstanding skill and beauty. The choir was elegantly dressed and sang with great passion. Several times throughout the performance, I was moved to tears.

Every seat in the beautiful auditorium was filled. A man was sitting on my left; Terry was on my right. A woman was sitting beside him, along with her husband on the end of the aisle. While we were carried away with the music and the singing, the woman sitting beside Terry was napping. While she was snoozing, Terry said that he thought I was wanting to get very close to him. What he did not know was that I was moving closer to him because the man beside me was falling asleep. He kept leaning closer and closer until he was leaning on my shoulder! I was shocked that they could sleep at such a wonderful and beautiful event.

After over an hour of amazing music, there was an intermission. Most everyone in the audience took a brief break and walked around to stretch their legs or purchase a refreshment.

After the intermission, Terry and I enthusiastically made our way back to our seats. However, the others on our row didn't return after the intermission. We had the row to ourselves. I found it unusual that people would want to leave such a fantastic event.

As the concert ended, we all stood to our feet and began to applaud. The applause was thunderous and continued on for quite some time. As the applause began to wane, I followed suit. Then, the clapping started again, from one side of the magnificent building to the other. It was a new and energized applause, greater than the previous round. This pattern continued several times.

As I stood there, applauding with such energy, I began to realize that I was giving some pretty extravagant praise to the musicians and singers I had just heard. I also realized that I usually did not give that much energy and extravagance in my praise when I would stand in God's presence at our church services. I was moved to tears at that moment, not from the music, but from my conviction that I should be

Week Forty-Two: Symphony

more passionate in my own worship to our Lord. He is the creator of the universe. He is the healer of my heart. He is the Savior of my soul. He is the giver of eternal life. He is my Father, my guide, my Redeemer, and my King. I must not forget that He is everything to me. He is worthy of my highest, most sincere, and most passionate worship. I will praise Him, and give Him glory. Will you join me in a renewed decision to sincerely worship Him with your best?

"Honor the Lord for the glory of his name. Worship the Lord in the splendor of his holiness" (Psalm 29:2).

Joy for Life

WEEK FORTY-THREE

Texting

I love the convenience of texting. It's great, but I deal with two issues: First, I'm usually in a hurry, and second, I'm a spelling nut. Those things, coupled with the convenience of texting, do not always make for a good mix. For example, I often end a text with, "We love you guys." More times than I like to remember, the "Y" was turned into a "T" and, "We love you guys," was sent stating, "We love you guts." Even though I usually caught the mistake right away after sending, it was still sent and there was no retrieving it. How embarrassing! Has that ever happened to you? If you text regularly, you don't have to answer that. I already know the answer!

Yes, we all make mistakes. We are human. I'm thankful that my friends and family who received the text, "We love you guts," recognized the intent of my greeting. Hopefully, they even got a laugh out of it. Thankfully, I have not lost a relationship over my spelling errors in a text.

When I read the words of Christ, there is no question that He loves us. There is no question about His authority.

Joy for Life

When I read the words of Christ, there is no question about His death on a cross to save me. There is no question about His resurrection and His power over death and the grave. His words are powerful. His words have shaped and guided my life.

John 6:63 says,
> The Spirit gives eternal life. Human effort accomplishes nothing. And the very words I have spoken to you are the spirit and life.

The words of Christ are life to us in our crazy world of chaos and uncertainty. When the news in the world around me is disturbing, I can go to the words of Christ and find peace and hope. When my physical body is tired and in pain, I can go to the words of Christ and find strength and healing. When my mind is troubled, I can go to the words of Christ and find serenity and calm. When my heart is dry and thirsty, I can go to the words of Christ and find refreshing for my soul.

The words of Christ are powerful. The Word of God is powerful. Every day, I can find strength in His Word. Whatever we have need of, His Word addresses it. I'm thankful for the Word of God. No mistakes. No errors. No, *Oops, I didn't mean to send that.* His words are truth and life. That knowledge makes me happy.

I love you guts! Oops…I mean you guys!

WEEK FORTY-FOUR

The Abandoned Raft

Terry and I recently enjoyed going on a cruise. It was such a marvelous experience, and we were blessed in so many ways as we enjoyed the beauty of God's creation. I will be talking about it over and over again, I'm sure.

One morning of the cruise, there was an announcement made over the ship's speakers. The captain had shifted direction momentarily to inspect a damaged vessel that was close by. They assured the passengers that it would be a brief diversion, and that we would still be arriving at our next port on schedule. Our curiosity was aroused. Many of us on board the ship made our way to an area where we could look over the side of the ship and see this vessel that had caused a diversion. There it was out in the vast, open ocean. It was a tiny vessel, obviously homemade, not much more than a raft-like little boat. It was made of small pieces of wood and had Styrofoam all tied together to keep it afloat. It had a makeshift sail of sorts extending upward. There were water bottles hanging around the edges of the little boat. It had what appeared to be piles of towels or rags of some kind. However, there was no person in or around it. As many of us stood on the side and watched the little boat bouncing on the ocean, everyone began to talk about the origin of it. Had it come from Cuba? Had it come with an individual, or maybe a small family trying to make an escape from where they were, hoping to find a better place? We all expressed hope that perhaps it was uninhabited because they had been rescued by another ship already, and the little homemade raft-boat was just abandoned. We all expressed hope that they were rescued, not lost at sea.

I couldn't forget the little raft, and kept wondering who made it and why. It obviously appeared to be a scene of desperation. Someone, somewhere, was so desperate to leave, they would risk sailing across miles and miles of ocean to find another shore. I will never know if they were rescued or if they lost their life in the deep waters of the ocean in their desperation.

As I ponder about that, I realize that there are people all around us that are desperate. I'm not talking about the ones in Cuba, building a little raft-boat to sail the ocean in hopes of rescue. The ones I'm thinking about are drowning in an ocean just the same. Their ocean may be depression, or bondage to sinful pleasures. They may be sailing in an ocean of unforgiveness or anger in a little raft of their own making, and they will never survive the mighty ocean waves on their own. They are not in Cuba, but they may be in Texas or Florida or even Arizona, with no real ocean for miles around. They are in need of rescue. They are in need of someone to divert their own vessel of safety and security, and take the time to save someone who is about to perish in the deep waters of a troubled sea.

When the sea is troubled, there is only one who speaks peace to the troubled sea. There is only one who has ever just spoken the word and the sea obeyed His commands. When we call on that one, who is Jesus Christ, He can calm the sea, rescue the desperate ones, and bring hope and healing. When we yield our lives to Him, He can rescue us from those deep, dark ocean waters of depression, unforgiveness, or bondage. He is the one!

> And He arose, and rebuked the wind, and said unto the sea, 'Peace, be still.' And the wind ceased, and there was a great calm (Mark 4:39 KJV).

Joy for Life

WEEK FORTY-FIVE

The Broken Cup

Psalm 51:17 says, "The sacrifice you desire is a broken spirit. You will not reject a broken and repentant heart, O God."

For a number of years, I collected beautiful teacups. I have enjoyed sharing with friends how I acquired each one. Some have been given to me by our daughters, from my mother, or by other family members and friends. Some of the teacups are old and have come from antique stores in various states. I have some teacups from England given to me by a friend. She shared interesting stories with me about where the teacups came from. I enjoy looking at each one, sharing a cup of tea with someone, or having a tea party on occasion. Every now and then, when I have found one that I really wanted, I have purchased it for myself to add to the collection.

Just after Christmas, I was in the dining room, carefully packing away our Christmas decorations, knowing it would likely be another eleven months or so before I unpack these items. After putting everything away in the attic, I continued cleaning. I was enjoying myself, cleaning mirrors, dusting shelves and furniture. I decided to clean several of my prized teacups that were displayed on a wooden shelf that one of my sons-in-law made for me many years ago.

Although I was carefully moving the cups for cleaning and polishing the shelf, my arm bumped one, knocking it to the ceramic tile floor. It shattered! I was sad to see my beautiful Blue Willow teacup in many pieces on the floor, obviously beyond repair. I quickly calmed myself, and was glad that it was one I had purchased for myself, not a treasured gift from a loved one.

I began to sweep up the pieces, and feeling very bad that it had shattered. I was thinking I would just throw the pieces away. Then I remembered that I have seen some beautiful jewelry at craft shows made from pieces of a broken teacup. The colors and designs are so beautiful, but the pieces just have to be formed in an appropriate shape and size for making a necklace or earrings. I could not bear to just throw the pieces away, so I have tucked them away for future use. Who knows, maybe I will take up jewelry making someday!

As I looked at the pieces of the teacup, I realized that in some ways a teacup is similar to life. God has lovingly created, molded, and shaped us. Every one of us are wonderful, unique creations of our God. There are times that we fall, are knocked down, or knocked over. We may feel that we are shattered into many pieces. Sometimes, we think we are broken beyond repair. But our loving God, the creator of the universe, the Almighty One, is there to pick up the broken pieces, and puts us back together again. He is so loving. He makes us better than new. The refining process is not easy, but God is tender, loving, and gently shows His faithfulness to us time and again. He will not reject a broken and repentant heart.

Joy for Life

WEEK FORTY-SIX

The Powerful Word of God

I love to read. I am particularly interested in biographies, stories of history, and actual events. I am fascinated when I read the stories of how God uses people through the generations to make a difference in the world. I grew up hearing the stories about the heroes of faith in the Bible, and still love to read about and hear their stories of provision, faith, miracles, and so much more.

I read about a United States Air Force soldier who was captured and held as a Vietnam prisoner of war for seven years. He told how he attended church regularly the first eighteen years of his life, but had not really considered a relationship with Christ a top priority until his capture as a POW. In his story, he said he began to try to remember verses and hymns he knew, as well as sermons he had heard. Remembering those things is the only thing that helped him survive those seven horrible years. Throughout the prison camp, he and some of the other prisoners would try to put together the Bible verses they could remember. Most of them could remember the 23rd Psalm, and the Lord's Prayer. But he said the camp favorite, by far, was

John 3:16. He said during that time, he knew he could never be without a Bible throughout the remainder of his life, because it was God's Word that kept him alive.

In thinking about his story, I thought how significant the people were that taught him those verses, preached those sermons, and sang those songs that helped carry him through seven years as a prisoner. They made a powerful impact on that young man, and their teaching and training literally helped keep him alive during that difficult time.

I love to read about others who have made a difference in the lives of people through their teaching or training. I love to read about those whose ministries have impacted people with God's love. I'm captivated by the stories of people who make history with their amazing dedication to do things like discover new medical cures or become astronauts. God uses so many people to accomplish great and wonderful things.

He is using you to accomplish something great for Him. Yes, I said He is using you to accomplish greatness! Think about it—whose lives are you impacting for Him? What difference have you made in someone's life? Who are the people in your own sphere of influence? We all influence many other people and we all make a difference. We must choose to be a positive influence. We must choose to make a powerful and significant difference to those we have opportunity to impact. I'm convinced that none of us know the far-reaching influence that we have on so many lives. It is a privilege that we have been given by God to impact our world for His glory and His purpose.

You may be the key to the survival for someone when they are in their prison, or when they are fighting their war spiritually. God has a great purpose for each one of us. I want to be sure I am accomplishing the purpose He has for me. One of those wonderful stories I remember from God's Word is about Esther, who realized she had been strategically placed for God's purpose. Esther 4:14 says, "…and who knoweth whether thou art come to the kingdom for such a time as this?" (KJV).

God loves you and has a great plan and purpose for you!

Joy for Life

WEEK FORTY-SEVEN

The Statistics Tell Us

Call me crazy, but I love statistics and the whole idea of analytics. I enjoy putting together papers with statistics of one kind or another. I have always thought that was a good thing.

But as I think about Jesus and the way He reached people, I don't see once where He used statistics like I tend to use. I don't see where He indicated, *20% of my disciples will do 80% of the work in the Kingdom.* I don't see where He told the 5,000 hungry people, *I see that 62% of you hungry people are not disciples, so I'm going to feed you and ask you to follow me.* He just fed the hungry people.

What I *do* see Jesus communicating to people are simple stories that they will understand. He speaks to them about farming. He speaks to them about fishing. He speaks to them about sheep, and He shares the gospel by talking about things they understand. He doesn't try to move them with statistics.

I need to be more like Jesus. When I see my harvest field, I want to see people as Jesus sees them. Maybe instead of knowing so many statistics, I need to think about what will reach someone. Maybe it will be talking about music, cooking, or parenting. Maybe it will be talking about a good book I just read. Maybe I should learn more about what's happening in their lives instead of analyzing why they are in the "46% of Americans who have dealt with that issue."

I'm going to do better. I'm 99% sure of it!

WEEK FORTY-EIGHT

To Tell the Truth

As I was driving in to work last Monday, I was listening to a radio commentator. Conservative radio talk show hosts so often emphasize that they are telling the truth. I will admit, with all of the news and all the commentaries we hear, how can we know what is totally the truth?

John 8:31-32 says,

> Jesus said to the people who believed in him, "You are truly my disciples if you remain faithful to my teachings. And you will know the truth, and the truth will set you free."

Recently I interviewed a candidate for a job. I was going through my interview routine, asking the questions I typically ask, noting my observations throughout the process. After discussion of the job responsibilities, I asked the candidate what strengths she thought she possessed that would be of benefit to our organization. She hesitated a few moments. I thought I would help her out, and I shared with her that usually when I ask this question, a candidate will tell me that they are dependable or loyal.

They might say they have integrity. Sometimes they will let me know they are a fast learner, or very easy to get along with—standard good qualities that one might perceive an employer was looking for. After explaining this, I asked her, "Are you dependable?" She quickly said, "Yes, I am." I asked, "Are you honest?" To my surprise, she answered, "Yes, when I need to be." I was so shocked by the answer, I responded without hesitation. Looking directly at her I said, "That is not a good answer. You are either honest or you're not. If you are not honest, that is a character flaw." I think she knew then that her chances for being hired were absolutely zero. Honesty is important in every aspect of our lives. Telling the truth is important.

I love God's Word, because it is truth. There is no doubt. His Word declares the truth!

> Jesus told him, "I am the way, the truth, and the life. No one can come to the Father except through me" (John 14:6).
>
> Jesus replied, "I tell you the truth, unless you are born again, you cannot see the Kingdom of God" (John 3:3).
>
> For God so loved the world that he gave his one and only Son, that whoever believes in him shall not perish but have eternal life (John 3:16 NIV).

I'm so thankful for the promise of God. I'm thankful that "whosoever" includes me. I'm thankful that as a young child of six years old, I received Christ as my Savior and Redeemer, asked Him to forgive my sins, and come into my heart. I was born again.

I'm so thankful that the truth sets us free. I'm free from

condemnation. I'm free from fear. I'm free from the past, and free to move forward in victory and in confidence. I'm free to love, forgive, and so much more.

> If we claim to have fellowship with Him yet walk in the darkness, we lie and do not live by the truth. But if we walk in the light, as He is in the light, we have fellowship with one another, and the blood of Jesus, His Son, purifies us from all sin. If we claim to be without sin, we deceive ourselves and the truth is not in us. If we confess our sins, he is faithful and just and will forgive us our sins and purify us from all unrighteousness (I John 1:6-9 NIV).

My prayer—*Thank you, Lord Jesus, for forgiving my sins and providing freedom for me through the shedding of your precious blood. Thank you for truth. I'm thankful for the truth of Your love, Your grace and forgiveness, and the truth of eternal life that I have through Christ. Thank you for loving me, and knowing my every thought, word, and intent of my heart. Nothing is hidden from You. I love and adore You.*

Joy for Life

Week Forty-Nine

Toastmasters

For several years, I was a member of Toastmasters, a worldwide organization that empowers people to become more effective communicators and leaders. It helps people learn to get over the fear of public speaking and attempts to hone their speaking skills. Our Toastmasters Club met once per week, and we had quite a diverse membership. We had military officers, enlisted personnel, and civilians. I served as an officer in the club for multiple terms. It was a great experience. Our weekly club meetings were very structured. Each week, someone in the club was assigned to make a speech of an assigned type and length. Other members in the club were given jobs as the timekeeper or grammarian, and three people were assigned to be the evaluators of the speech. At the end of the speech, all of these people gave their evaluation, pointing out the shortcomings, as well as giving encouragement about the positive aspects of each one. The grammarian would point out all the grammatical errors of the speech. For example, if someone said, "I seen the car drive by," they would point out that the appropriate grammar was, "I saw the car drive

Joy for Life

by." We also had someone that was called the bell-ringer. Their job was to ding a bell each time the speaker would say something incorrect, or use a filler word, such as "uh" or "um." When the bell would ring, it was an interruption. If the bell rang many times during a speech, it could be embarrassing to the speaker. Having a bell ring every time you say something like "and, uh" certainly makes you stop and think before you speak. It was a great way, in a friendly, helpful environment, to learn to speak more effectively.

Now, let's think about that in spiritual terms. How effective are we in our Christian walk and talk? Are we saying the right things? Are we speaking words of faith and hope? Are we speaking words of truth and righteousness? How often would that bell ring if there was a someone who rang a little bell every time we said something that did not line up with God's Word? For example, if we said, *I guess God has forgotten where I am*, a bell would ring and the correction would be given to us: "For God has said, 'I will never fail you. I will never abandon you,'" (Hebrews 13:5). If we said, *I cannot do this. It's too much for me. I'm just too weak*, the bell would ring and the correction would be given: "I can do everything through Christ, who gives me strength" (Philippians 4:13). If we said, *I'm a loser and nobody cares anyway*, the bell would ring and the correction would be given:

> "For I know the plans I have for you," says the Lord. "They are plans for good and not for disaster, to give you a future and a hope. In those days when you pray, I will listen.

If you look for me wholeheartedly, you will find me" (Jeremiah 29:11-13).

The list could go on and on. If we could just hear that bell ring as a reminder to correct our thoughts and speech, it would help us begin to think. We would stop and think about the promises of God that are written to bring us hope and salvation. We would stop and think about the promises of God that bring healing and comfort to our hurts. We would stop and think about the promises of God that bring guidance and direction to our decisions.

After being in Toastmasters, there are still times I can hear that bell ring in my mind when I find myself saying, "Well, uh, I'm not sure, and-uh, I'll look into it." I don't want to hear that bell ring because I said the wrong thing. I want to say not only what is grammatically correct, but I want to say what is spiritually correct and in line with God's Word.

Joy for Life

WEEK FIFTY

Unexpected Surprise

Surprise! I think we've all heard this exciting word at some time in our lives. Maybe it was a birthday party someone planned, and everyone came out of hiding and screamed it at once. I've communicated it a few times in a conversation, as I've handed someone a gift and quietly said "It's a surprise!" I'm sure it's been used many times at the announcement of a grandchild, a new car, or just an unannounced visit. Whatever the case, I think we've all had a surprise at one time or another.

Our daughters reminded me earlier this year of a particular surprise I gave them a few years back. We were pastoring a small church. Finances were tight as could be. I tried to be creative with meals, but it was a challenge. One evening, I had prepared some vegetables, and created a main dish casserole with macaroni and cheese. The family asked what we were having, and I told them it was called hamburger surprise. When they started dishing out the main dish, one of the girls said, "I don't see any hamburger." I quickly replied, "That's the surprise!" We all got a good laugh out of our hamburger-less hamburger surprise.

Joy for Life

I've been seeing announcements about unclaimed money in Texas, and how everyone should check a certain website to see if they have anything in this special state fund. I have checked in years past, and actually found my name, but never with an address that matched any of my addresses. Much to my surprise, last week, I found my name, along with a valid address of mine. When I saw it, I could not believe it. Of course, since they advertise that millions of dollars are in these unclaimed pools of money, I became a bit excited. Even though I could not imagine ever having left money unclaimed, I tried to think of what it could possibly be. Maybe an old utility deposit, or bank account I thought was closed, or funds from insurance companies, or refunds and such. With great anticipation, I began to open the documents and found that I have an unclaimed amount of $6.20. I will be getting my check for this bounty in four to six weeks. That was a surprise!

We are all surprised at different times and at different things. Sometimes the surprise is in what God is doing and how He is using us. We expect things to happen a certain way, and we are surprised when they happen differently. We do not always see it. We certainly do not always understand it, but He is using us, His children, to do His work in this hurting world we live in. I am often surprised at things that happen, and then I realize that it is God's hand at work.

I recently read the Old Testament story about Naaman and how he wanted to be healed from leprosy. He expected a big ordeal from the prophet Elisha, and he expected that

Week Fifty: Unexpected Surprise

he would receive special attention. He became angry when the prophet sent a message for him to dip in the Jordan River seven times. Read 2 Kings 5:11-14, "But Naaman became angry and stalked away. 'I thought he would certainly come out to meet me!' he said. 'I expected him to wave his hand over the leprosy and call on the name of the Lord his God and heal me!' So Naaman turned and went away in a rage. But his officers tried to reason with him and said, 'Sir, if the prophet had told you to do something very difficult, wouldn't you have done it? So you should certainly obey him when he says simply, "Go and wash and be cured!"' So Naaman went down to the Jordan River and dipped himself seven times, as the man of God had instructed him. And his skin became as healthy as the skin of a young child's, and he was healed!"

What a surprise Naaman received, when simple obedience brought his cure and healing. He thought it would be some flamboyant event, and that he would certainly receive attention from the prophet. He could not imagine that seven dips in the river would cure his leprosy, but he obeyed and received what he had need of. What a surprise!

Surprises are all around us. Keep your eyes open. You'll most likely be surprised when you see what God has in store.

Joy for Life

WEEK FIFTY-ONE

What a Difference a Day Makes

What a difference a day makes! I've heard that saying many times through the years. It is true for all of us. As I think about some of the difference-making days of my life, I realize once again how absolutely magnificent God has been to me. Think about your own life for a few moments and how one day, just one event can change your life forever.

I love to think about those difference-making days that have brought such joy to my life: The day I received Christ into my heart; the day I got married to my remarkable husband; the day I became a mother to our beautiful daughter; the day I became a mother for the second time to another beautiful daughter; the two days I became a mother-in-love to the two fine young men that our daughters married; the day I became a grandmother to our first amazing grandson, multiplied by six wonderful days at the birth of our other grandsons. Yes, the list goes on and on. Those are the days of joyful celebration, those difference-making days. I love to think about those wonderful days that truly changed my life in a happy way.

There are also days that made a difference that are not joyful. I had days of pain and suffering through losing a baby. I've experienced days of mourning the loss of dear loved ones who left this earth much too soon, through horrible violence and tragedy, or from sickness and disease. How my heart aches when I think about those days that made a difference and changed our lives.

What a difference a day makes. It is true for me, and it is true for you. As long as we are alive, those days will keep coming. There will be days we hear great news that brings a smile to our face or laughter to our lives. There will also be days we hear a bad report from the doctor, gripping our hearts with fear; or we will hear sad news, bringing tears to our eyes and an ache to our heart.

There is something all the days, both good and bad, have in common. The common thread in it all, in joy or pain, is that we are never alone. Christ is with us through it all. When I think about the days of joy, I know without a doubt that Christ joined me in my rejoicing. When I think about the days of tragedy, I know without a doubt that He embraced me in my sorrow. He is the constant presence in every triumph and every tragedy. I find great comfort in knowing that I'm never alone, not even for one minute. He is there to hold me up and help me to keep on keeping on.

There was a day many years ago when Christ endured extreme rejection, merciless torture, and a cruel crucifixion, ending in an unfathomable death. It was a day of despair for His followers. But what a difference a day makes, when on the third day He arose, overcoming death and the grave. Now *that* day made the difference for all of us, and for eternity! When I'm overcome with heartache, sadness, or grief, I remember the resurrection of Christ. What victory and what amazing hope we have because of His resurrection.

I'm full of joy, filled with hope, and overflowing with anticipation. He's alive! He's always with me.

Joy for Life

WEEK FIFTY-TWO

Words Are Powerful

Words are so powerful! I'm going to mention a few words, and let's just see how powerful they are.

Vacation—Beach—Music—Sunshine—Happy—Joyful—Laughter

Now, don't you just feel better after reading those words?

Let's try some more ...

Fear—Floods—Nausea—Wreck—Tests—Broken—Sickness

Hmmm...not feeling so good now?

We all speak. Therefore, we all use many words every day. If words are powerful, and we know they are, then that means that you have power daily.

Terry and I made a decision early in our marriage that we would never say the words *shut up* to each other. When we had children, that decision remained constant. We just didn't do it. When our children were very small, a particular church we were pastoring had a children's church leader,

Joy for Life

who I will call "Buck." Buck had a nephew in the children's group named Jason. We noticed our daughter, Michelle, just a toddler at the time, came home very distraught after Sunday service. We asked her what was wrong. She said "I thought Buck was a Christian, but he told Jason to shut up in class today!" It was obviously not acceptable to her to hear someone say *shut up* and then teach a Bible lesson. Their Christianity was in question in the eyes of a toddler. Although we find that story amusing, I wonder how many people are listening to my words, watching my actions, and making sure that I am what I claim to be.

As I think about how powerful words are, I examine myself. How am I using words? Do I use words as building blocks in someone's life, or do I use them to shatter or demolish? In thinking about my words over the past week, I had the opportunity to speak words of thanks to people. I had the opportunity to say prayers and encourage people in their faith. I had the opportunity to say kind things and make others feel valued, to compliment them on a job well done or a task completed. I also had the responsibility to take care of some pretty intense counseling with someone at work. I tried to be wise and kind. I pray my words gave life and hope. I think I also missed some opportunities to speak encouragement or give thanks along the way, but I will try to do better next week.

Psalm 19:14 says,

Let the words of my mouth, and the meditation of my

Week Fifty-Two: Words Are Powerful

heart, be acceptable in thy sight, O Lord, my Strength, and my Redeemer (KJV).

Kind words are like honey—sweet to the soul and healthy for the body (Proverbs 16:24).

Joy for Life

About the Author

Connie Cross has a passion for encouraging others in their walk with God. She was raised in a pastor's home and has been involved in church since childhood. She actively serves along side her husband, Terry, a pastor and church planter for over 40 years. Connie and Terry, through In-Courage Ministries, have dedicated much of their time to encouraging pastors and their families to follow Christ and to fulfill their mission with joy. They currently pastor the Walnut Creek Church of God in Mansfield, Texas.

Connie is passionate about her love for her family. She and Terry have two daughters, Michelle Beth (and husband Gabe) and Amber Janelle (and husband Paul).

Joy for Life

They also have seven grandsons that bring such pride and joy—Zachary, Aiden, Spencer, Jacob, Joseph, Joshua, and Jonathan. She is always glad to show her latest photos and talk about the news from the grandsons.

A licensed minister of music in the Church of God, Connie has played the piano for camp meetings, state and national women's conferences, and General Assembly services. She has been a guest speaker, musician, and vocalist for women's events at churches throughout Texas.

In addition to her life of family and ministry, Connie has a 27 year career in medical research management, providing additional opportunities for travel and personal ministry. She is the vice president of a vascular surgery management group headquartered in Los Angeles. She has been a guest speaker for clinical research meetings in Chicago, Baltimore, Denver, San Antonio, New York, San Diego, and Nashville.

To contact Connie by email, write her at conniebcross@gmail.com.